CADBOROSAURUS

CADBOROSAURUS
SURVIVOR from the DEEP

BY

Paul H. LeBlond and Edward L. Bousfield

Horsdal & Schubart

Horsdal & Schubart Publishers Ltd.
Victoria, B.C., Canada

Cover painting by Susan Laurie-Bourque, Hull, P.Q.

This book is set in New Baskerville Book Text.

Printed and bound in Canada by Hignell Printing Limited, Winnipeg.

Canadian Cataloguing in Publication Data

LeBlond, P. H.
Cadborosaurus

Includes bibliographical references and index.
ISBN 0-920663-33-8

1. Cadborosaurus. I. Bousfield, E. L. II. Title.
QL89.2.C32L42 1995   001.9'44   C95-910282-5

DEDICATION

This book is dedicated to Bernard Heuvelmans, the father of cryptozoology, who chose an eccentric path while insisting on scientific rigour. He provided the original inspiration for this enquiry.

ACKNOWLEDGEMENTS

We wish to thank all those who have supported us in our belief that Cadborosaurus is a worthwhile topic of scientific investigation: John Sibert, who was into this from the very beginning; George Pickard, who, as director of what was then the Institute of Oceanography at the University of British Columbia, did not frown on a junior faculty member's eccentric hobby and even allowed publication of early results as part of the institute's Manuscript Report series; Bernard Heuvelmans, whose work inspired this interest and who received our early efforts with sympathy; Paul Stoddart, who patiently searched through newspaper archives; Gary Mangiacopra, John Green and John Grissim for their generosity in sharing information; Richard Greenwell, Roy Mackal and fellow members of the International Society of Cryptozoology for their continuing encouragement. We also remember that Paul Tennant first drew our attention to the Skagit River *atlatl*, and Grant Keddie played an important role in exhuming the Naden Harbour photograph from the B.C. Provincial Archives, and bringing it to our attention. We also thank Joan Thornley, at the Vancouver Maritime Museum, who dug up the G.V. Boorman photographs.

In the preparation of this book, we are deeply indebted to those who shared their personal experience of Caddy with us, who took part in our recent "Caddy watches" and field work around the Saanich Peninsula and San Juan Islands, and whose names appear in these pages. We value the help of those who have facilitated and promoted these informative contacts, particularly Patrick Murphy, city editor of the Victoria *Times-Colonist*. We are especially grateful to Kenneth Wills of Victoria for having made the scrapbook of his late father, Archie H. Wills, former editor of the *Victoria Daily Times*, available to us. We have valued similarly a Caddy scrapbook compiled by the late G. Clifford Carl, former director of the Royal British Columbia Museum; both have been precious sources of information and illustrations. We acknowledge the assistance of Captain William Hagelund, of Burnaby, and Mr. James Wakelen and Mr. Winston Garcin, both of Victoria, who provided first-hand information, background, and illustrative material concerning the Naden Harbour carcass, and confirmed the authenticity of pertinent photographs taken by the late F.S. Huband, former manager of the Naden Harbour whaling station.

We have discussed the subject matter of this book, and particularly the zoological interpretation of Caddy, with many professional colleagues, all of whom lent a sympathetic ear, and provided useful critical commentary and study references, even when sometimes disagreeing with our overall interpretation. We owe special thanks to Cas Lindsey and Al Lewis at the University of British Columbia who supported the study and urged a formal scientific description of the animal as a new species, and to Ian McTaggart-Cowan, of Victoria, who provided personal insights into the Caddy events of the late 1930s at the Royal B.C. Museum. We are also grateful for the professional interest and review support of Dale Russell, Canadian Museum of Nature, Ottawa; Chris McGowan, Royal Ontario Museum, Toronto; Derek V. Ellis, University of Victoria; and Francis R. Cook, editor of *The Canadian Field Naturalist* and former Dominion Herpetologist at the Canadian Museum of Nature. To all our friends and supporters, and to members of the B.C. Scientific Cryptozoology Club, we extend our warmest thanks.

Finally, we are most grateful to Marlyn Horsdal for her help and patience in guiding us towards a final manuscript.

CONTENTS

DEDICATION
ACKNOWLEDGEMENTS
INTRODUCTION
CHAPTER I   EARLY GLIMPSES   1
CHAPTER II   FRONT-PAGE NEWS!   14
CHAPTER III   A CONTINUING PRESENCE   26
CHAPTER IV   ON THE BEACH   45
CHAPTER V   JOKES AND HOAXES   60
CHAPTER VI   WHAT IS CADDY?   69
CHAPTER VII   CADDY'S COUSINS   84
CHAPTER VIII   WHAT NEXT?   89
APPENDIX I   LIST OF CADDY SIGHTINGS   93
APPENDIX II   STRANDINGS/CAPTURES   119
FOOTNOTES   122
BIBLIOGRAPHY   128
INDEX   132

This book is about Caddy, British Columbia's sea-serpent. Although reported by hundreds of eyewitnesses over the past century, this animal remains a "cryptid": a creature whose existence is still in doubt because of insufficient material evidence.

The evidence for Caddy consists mostly of eyewitness descriptions, often accompanied by original sketches. Depictions of Caddy-like creatures have also been found among native artifacts. In addition, a solidly authenticated, otherwise unidentified, carcass has been postulated to be a juvenile Caddy. Besides reviewing the evidence, extensively and critically, we offer here a zoological explanation for Caddy.

Cryptozoology, a term coined by Bernard Heuvelmans in the 1960s, is the scientific study of hidden animals, i.e. animals about which only testimonial evidence is available, or material evidence considered insufficient by some.[1] These animals are often called "cryptids", a more neutral term than "monsters". Cryptozoology is a controversial field, strewn with logical pitfalls. Before venturing into it, we will see where it fits within the broader realm of natural history.

The discovery and classification of new animals used to be the central preoccupation of zoologists. Naturalists accompanied major expeditions, returning home with samples, descriptions and stories of new creatures. Efforts to make sense of the diversity of the world's fauna led to the idea of evolution. Today, the focus of biological research has shifted towards the explanation of the mechanisms of life. Nevertheless, new animals continue to be discovered. While most of these are insects and other small creatures, larger animals occasionally turn up, in mountainous areas or in the oceans. Over 50 years ago, the capture of a living coela-

canth, a fish-like animal thought to be ancestral to all land vertebrates, and known only from the fossil record, caused a major
sensation.[2] In contrast, the discovery of the megamouth shark,
without known fossil antecedents, caused hardly a ripple in the
world of marine science.[3] These discoveries have left in their wake
a presumption that other marine animals might be found. It is
more difficult to understand how large animals could have
remained hidden on land. Nevertheless, quite recently, a new
bovid, the Vu Quang ox, was found in the forests of Vietnam.[4]

New animals are sometimes found entirely unexpectedly: such was
the case of the coelacanth and the megamouth shark. No one had
reported seeing them; no one was looking for them. Sometimes,
however, vague reports precede discovery. The legend of the Kraken
was part of Nordic folklore for centuries before the discovery and
identification of the giant squid, *Architeuthis*.[5] Stories of the gorilla
came to the ears of European scientists long before they actually saw
one.[6] Hunters' stories led to the search for the Vu Quang ox.

In the period between first reports and scientific description,
there is not enough evidence, usually for lack of a specimen, to
ensure full acceptance of a new creature. That period is the realm
of cryptozoology. Driven by relentless curiosity, cryptozoologists
seek additional clues to confirm or deny the existence of elusive
cryptids. Because it focusses on the most fundamental of scientific
questions, that of existence, cryptozoology is fuelled by the basic
spirit of discovery which is the mainspring of science. One should
then not wonder at the breadth of its popular appeal. However,
because of its aura of uncertainty, cryptozoology can be a source of
continuous frustration for a mind insisting on logical certitude.
New bits of evidence are rarely decisive and theoretical arguments
usually remain unconvincing, so that final judgment must long be
held in abeyance. It is the search that is exciting: after a while,
actual discovery becomes almost secondary.

This book presents the evidence for Caddy. Either all the
evidence is to be rejected as insufficient, or there really still roams in
the waters of the North Pacific a large, undiscovered marine
creature. Somewhere in between lies the realm of cryptozoology. By
the time you are done, dear reader, you will know as much as we do
about this mysterious cryptid and you will be able to arrive at your
own answer to the fundamental question: Does Caddy really exist?

CHAPTER I

EARLY GLIMPSES

"To actually see an actual marine monster
Is one of the things that to do before I die I wonster."

Ogden Nash
"Dragons Are Too Seldom Seen"

An Unexpected Encounter

Dungeness Spit is a long finger of sand that juts out into Juan de Fuca Strait, near the entrance of Puget Sound; it is an exciting place to walk by the sea, to watch freighters bound for Seattle and Tacoma, and to observe waves and sea life. On a clear day, the mountains of Vancouver Island are visible to the north; snow-capped, volcanic Mount Baker towers on the mainland to the east. On a mid-March afternoon in 1961, Margaret Stout was strolling along the spit with her sister-in-law, Mrs. Fred Parson, and their small sons, aged four and five.

"It was a dark, drizzly and quiet day," she wrote. "We could see Vancouver Island vaguely through the mist. Ships in the channel were easily visible. We were at the beginning [western end] of the spit. We were watching a large freighter far out in the channel. It was moving up the Strait towards Port Townsend. When it was about 45° northeast of us, our atten-

1

tion was drawn to a long thin object about 25° northeast and probably a quarter of a mile from us. At first, we thought it was a tree limb. It disappeared abruptly beneath the surface and in a few seconds appeared again, much closer. We could see that it was some kind of creature and distinctly saw that the large flattish head was turned away from us and towards the ship. I think all of us gasped and pointed. We could distinctly see three humps behind the long neck. The animal was proceeding westward at an angle towards us. It sank abruptly again and reappeared closer, almost due north of us. In the dim light, we could distinctly make out colour and pattern, a long floppy mane, and the shape of the head. My small son grabbed me and started to cry with fear. At the same time, the animal seemed to become aware of us and sank again. It reappeared in a few seconds, still proceeding westwards, but a little way from us. I reassured the youngster, saying that it was obviously wary of us. It sank and reappeared once more while near enough to observe it closely. My sister-in-law is a good photographer and had her 35 mm camera. We had time to discuss that she should try to get a picture of it. She said the light was too poor and the background of the dull sea would not give any contrast. Mostly we were so busy exchanging notes and keeping track of the creature's progress that there was no time.

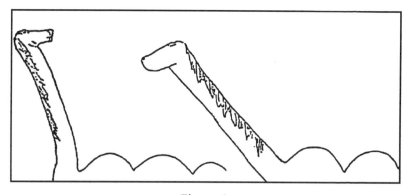

Figure 1.
Two views of Caddy, as seen by Margaret Stout and Mrs. F. Parson from Dungeness Spit, Juan de Fuca Strait, March 1961. (FROM LeBLOND AND SIBERT, 1973).

"As a trained biologist," she added, "including marine and fresh water biology, I could not accept that long floppy mane or fin. Yet we all saw it. We deduced that the humps were at least five feet. Again, I simply could not accept their arrangement." [1]

Well before the arrival of Europeans on the Pacific coast of North America, and repeatedly over the past century, people have seen strange, unidentifiable marine animals off the British Columbia and Washington coasts. Their experience has often resembled that of Margaret Stout and her relatives: a combination of surprise, fear, confusion and denial. Enough people have actually seen this creature that it has been given a name: Cadborosaurus, or Caddy, for short. For decades now, newspapers in coastal towns have reported these sightings, alternately championing or ridiculing Caddy's existence.

Everyone has heard of the Loch Ness monster; many will also have heard of Ogopogo, a large water creature supposed to inhabit Lake Okanagan, and perhaps also of Champ, the Lake Champlain monster. Other lakes in North America, Sweden, Russia and Japan are also believed to hide elusive water creatures. In addition, there have been hundreds of reports of "sea-monsters" or "sea-serpents" of various kinds, many being quite similar in description to Caddy.

The existence of such animals, as indeed of Caddy itself, has remained a subject of debate: the weight of evidence, consisting of numerous and detailed eyewitness reports, has not convinced skeptics who demand a specimen to examine. Nevertheless, there are strong clues that there may exist, especially in the oceans, where new animals continue to be discovered regularly, creatures glimpsed but not yet captured and recorded by science. Caddy is one of those cryptids, or undiscovered animals.

Caddy in Native Culture

If Caddy really exists, the native inhabitants of the British Columbia coast must have seen it too. Their legends should mention it; their artifacts would show its likeness. Animals discovered by "official" science are usually already familiar to natives. The famous coelacanth, whose discovery 50 years ago caused such excitement, was already well known to the natives of the Comoro

Islands, who caught it for food and even used its rough skin in the repair of bicycle inner tubes. If there is a Caddy, one would expect to find traces of it in native folklore.

There are many sea-serpent stories in west-coast native folklore. The Manhousat people, who live in the area of Flores Island and Sydney Inlet, on the west coast of Vancouver Island, called it "*hiyitl'iik*": he who moves by wriggling from side to side. According to Manhousat elder Luke Swan, "Sea-serpents were said to be about seven or eight feet long. They moved very quickly, both on land and on water. They had legs, but when travelling on land, used their bodies more than their legs for propulsion — moving like snakes." Sea-serpents were rarely seen, especially in recent times. Mr. Swan's father had once come upon one. He shot an arrow at it but missed. The sea-serpent could grow wings at will and "its head and back were covered with long hair, as is represented with strips of dyed red cedar bark on the sea-serpent mask."[2] Figure 2 provides a modern rendition of *hiyitl'iik*.

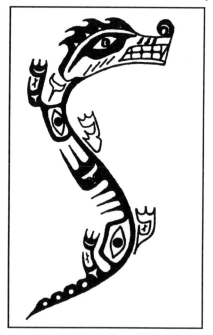

Figure 2.
The sea-serpent HIYITL'IIK. (FROM ELLIS AND SWAN, 1981).

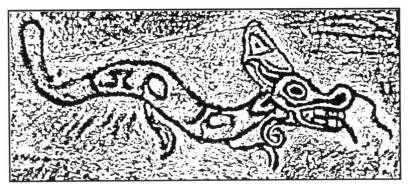

Figure 3.
Petroglyph from the Monsell site, Nanaimo River, B.C. (FROM HILL AND HILL, 1974).

On the Strait of Georgia, the Comox band, on Vancouver Island, spoke of the sea-monster *Numkse lee Kwala*, which they would watch for off Hornby Island. Comox elder Mary Clifton relates that on the way to Cape Mudge a very long sea-serpent was seen by her relatives. Apparently "it rose out of the water and then fell back with a loud crash. It was playful and didn't hurt any one of the number of people who saw it."[3] On the mainland coast of the strait, the Sechelt mythology spoke of appearances of a friendly, Caddy-like creature called *T'chain-ko.*[4]

Artifacts preserve shapes and forms which words may not always convey faithfully. At numerous sites along British Columbia shores, local artists or shamans scratched shallow engravings, called petroglyphs, in prominent rock faces. The full meaning of many of these icons has been lost; human faces, salmon, sun symbols, ships and other shapes can be recognized. Also, some of these petroglyph animals closely resemble *hiyitl'iik* of Manhousat lore.

For example, an animal from the Monsell site (Figure 3), beside the Nanaimo River, has a long, sinuous body, four small legs or flippers, prominent teeth, a big eye and some feature on its head (horns? a mane?). Another, from Gabriola Island, has very similar features, although no hind limbs are shown (Figure 4).

The representations of sea-monsters in native petroglyphs are striking in their consistency, which suggests that the carvers (or their close acquaintances) could have seen these creatures. There is no indication of scale in the petroglyphs, so no one can be sure that the animals represented are as large as those reported in the

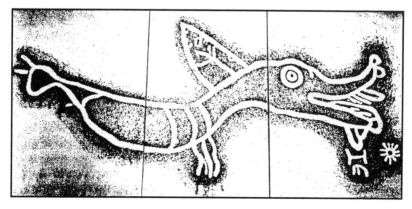

Figure 4.
Petroglyph from Gabriola Island. (FROM BENTLEY AND BENTLEY, 1981).

ocean. It is important to remember the presence of purely mythical creatures in west-coast Indian folklore, such as the thunderbird, for which no zoological basis has ever been suspected, and there is a possibility that the *hiyitl'iik* might also be such a mythical animal.

The Skagit River *atlatl* (spear-thrower) (Figure 5) is one of the best-known prehistoric Northwest Coast sculptures; it is currently in the collection of the University of British Columbia's Museum of Anthropology. This artifact has been dated at 1700 (+/-100) years before the present.[5] The *atlatl* is carved out of a single piece of western yew; the handle is carved in the shape of a human head surmounted by a sea-monster. This animal is quite reminiscent of that found in some petroglyphs; it has an open mouth full of square teeth, prominent eyes, two types of head appendages, possibly a crest and ears, and four limbs. The three-toed forelegs clasp the side of the head; the hind legs, also with three toes, are folded back along the tail. The tail is visible in the bottom panel; it has flat, whale-like flukes enclosing an open space (looking somewhat like a bottle opener). There are fins on the back. The curved lines at the top of the animal's neck have been interpreted alternately as skin folds or as gill slits. Four deeply incised lines divide the back into carapace-like segments. There are also deeply carved grooves on the side of the animal's body.

Is *hiyitl'iik*, as depicted in Manhousat legends, and in ancient artifacts, a representation of a real, live, yet still hidden, animal,

Figure 5.
The Skagit River ATLATL (spear thrower). (COURTESY UBC MUSEUM OF ANTHROPOLOGY).

(as cryptozoologists might claim) or of a mythical creature like the thunderbird? It is clear that, real or mythical, there existed a solid tradition in local folklore of a large sea-serpent which clearly antedates the arrival of European settlers, and which may be regarded as the earliest evidence for Caddy.

Early Settlers Also See Caddy

It did not take very long before European settlers began to report sea-serpent sightings. Their reports consist of testimonial evidence, contained in early documents and newspaper accounts. There are so many such sightings over the past century that to list every one of them would be tedious and repetitive. Only a few of the most striking and revealing observations have been selected for a detailed description. Readers thirsting for more information will find in Appendix I a chronological list of all sightings which satisfy two criteria. First of all there must be no doubt that what has been observed is truly an animal (not a log, or waves, for example); second, there must also be no doubt that the animal observed is of an unknown nature (not perhaps a seal, or a whale, or a beaver). Except in some very special cases, any sighting that does not satisfy these criteria has not been included in the data base. For example, a sighting by Vancouver Deputy Police Chief Harry Whelan was omitted; he claimed to have seen Caddy while fishing in Vancouver Harbour in 1952, but "couldn't tell whether it was the head or the back" that he saw of some unidentified "underwater thing".[6] The object of all the sightings is referred to as Caddy, for simplicity, though under this term there may hide more than one unknown creature and also perhaps some residual misinterpretation.

According to a 1940 obituary, Frank Stannard, a pioneer Nanaimo merchant, was one of the first British Columbia residents of European origin to glimpse Caddy. In the summer of 1881, Mr. Stannard, then a boy of 12, was one of a party of six young people who were paddling a canoe off William Head (near Race Rocks, Juan de Fuca Strait), when suddenly there rose beside them a monster of "unknown habits". Young Stannard pulled out his slingshot and let fly at one of the creature's "folds". The shot ricochetted off the serpent, which then dived below the surface.[7] No details; this is of interest mostly because it is the first observation on record.

A rather more detailed account of a surprising encounter which took place in the Queen Charlotte Islands on 26 June, 1897, was provided by prospector Osmond Fergusson. The description is contained in a letter found in the British Columbia Provincial Archives by archivist David Mattison. In Fergusson's words (the square brackets are Mattison's):

"About 4.30 this morning we left Caedoo [Kaidju?].[8] I was steering the boat and pushing an oar at the same time. There was no wind. The boat was 100 yards from shore, going south, with a fair tide. I saw ahead of us what I thought was a piece of drift wood. On getting closer, I noticed it was moving towards us. When within 50 yards, I said to Walker (my partner), What is that? It seems to be moving this way (against the tide). What we could see was an object like sketch (A) sticking out of the water about two feet. When within a few feet of it the end uncoiled and raised a long neck about five feet out of the water with a head like a snake['s] on it. The arched portion making a broad flat chest like I have seen on the cob[r]a I think.

"When the serpent or whatever it was saw us it turned slightly towards land to avoid the boat. The head and neck were almost immediat[e]ly put under water again. As it passed the boat, at a distance, that with an effort, I could have thrown a[n] oar on it we could see a body about 25 feet long tapering with a fish like tail and I think a continuous fin running the length of the body.

"A slow undulating motion went along the body, while the tail part had a steady sweep from side to side of about six feet. A curious thing was the broad neck or chest part that formed the arch (or hurricane dick, Walker called it). The only part out of water when the head was down was not exposed broadways in the direction the fish was going, but had a decided twist to the left allowing the water to flow through it."⁹

The description of this sighting (sketched in Figure 6) contains some of the elements which often crop up in such accounts: the witnesses' initial assumption that it was a familiar object ("I thought it was a piece of driftwood"); their surprise and confusion at the unfamiliarity of the creature; and their description of various features in terms of their resemblance to those of a known animal.

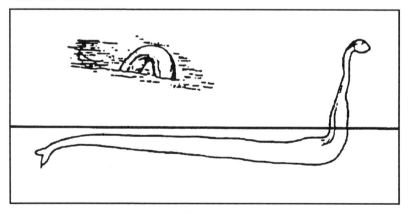

Figure 6.
The animal seen by Fergusson and Walker off the Queen Charlotte Islands in 1897. (FROM MATTISON, 1964).

Many of the early sightings reported here only came to light many years after they occurred. Witnesses were often fearful of the ridicule which accompanies unusual observations. Public interest following well-publicized sightings (as in October 1933), or scientific enquiries, brought old-time witnesses out of the closet. In response to a broadly advertised expression of interest in "sea-serpents" put out by Paul LeBlond and John Sibert in November 1969, a number of previously unreported sightings came to light. Philip H. Welch, then living in Port Alberni, sent in an interesting account.

In 1905 (or 1906 — he wasn't sure which year), Mr. Welch was working for logging contractor Herb Tomlinson on Cracroft Island (across Johnstone Strait east of northern Vancouver Island), barking logs for horse-team hauling. On a September Sunday, he and a workmate took the boss's 16-foot rowboat across Johnstone Strait to go trout fishing in the Adams River. When they got there, they discovered that there was an enormous run of pink salmon and that the river was so congested with salmon as to make it impossible to fish for trout. It was only about nine a.m. but the fishermen were resigned to having rowed in vain across the strait when less than half a mile from the mouth of the river, a long (six to eight feet) neck appeared, some 200 yards away from their boat. Welch wanted to shoot at the creature with his hunting rifle, but his companion persuaded him not to, for fear the creature would attack. While they were arguing, the creature submerged "with very little disturbance".

"We rowed hard for shore," Welch continued, "hitting many salmon with our oars as we moved in, and it again appeared this time about 100 yards astern." As the creature turned its head, looking up and down Johnstone Strait, they could observe that its neck was about the size of a stovepipe, tapering from a 20-inch diameter at the base to about ten inches at the head, which looked like a giraffe's. Welch noticed two bumps on the head, about five inches high and rounded on top. To him, the head did not look like that of a flesh-eating creature. The animal was brown; no hair or mane was visible. He remarked that although the animal was gaining on them, he could see no wake behind it. The animal again sank without disturbance and was not seen again.

Welch recalls that he was not scared, as he was sure he could "easily break its neck with the rifle", having "used a gun since the age of nine and having killed many deer and a bear or two". He also insists that there was "no possible chance of confusing this creature with sea lions, seals, porpoises, dolphins, whales or any known sea creature."[10]

It was in the same general area that Mrs. Hildegarde Forbes, on a steamer bound for Skagway, Alaska, in August 1912, saw a 40-foot-long, "definitely snake-like" creature. It had "its head raised and steady all the time it was in view; this was several minutes; dark, but not black; his mane seemed like seaweed; did not see eye, mouth, etc; he had a number of 'humps' (probably five to seven) which seemed to rise and fall as he moved. I did not get the impression that he had a large body," she concluded.[11]

Another observation to surface only years later is that of R.M. Elliott who saw a sea-serpent in July 1917 while working on the telegraph line between Jordan River and Port Renfrew. "I noticed an object about 200 yards out to sea," he wrote, "moving along at about three knots, heading for Jordan River and Victoria. It showed about eight feet of neck which, I should judge, was about two feet in diameter, resembling a giraffe's head and neck. As it swam, it appeared to be scrutinizing each side of the straits. The other portion of the body showing, indicated reptile formation, with four or five humps similar to those seen when a snake is swimming. I did not see any tail to it." Elliott then ran to his shack for his rifle, shot and hit the creature, which "jumped, exposing its exposed neck length to fifteen or sixteen feet, and lashed the water to such an extent that it reminded me of a steamer docking when a kick back or ahead is ordered. After it had quietened down a little it proceeded on its course, swaying its head from one side to the other."[12] Altogether, the animal was in sight for about three quarters of an hour, an unusually long observation period.

Without casting doubts on Elliott's observations, one should note here that swimming snakes do not show vertical "humps" any more than when they are slithering on the ground. It is not surprising, however, that many witnesses should associate undulating motion, even in the wrong plane, with snakes, since no other large animals move in such a fashion.

Another respondent to the LeBlond and Sibert survey was Cyril G. Cook, of Surrey, B.C. In his December 1969 letter, he described how, on a clear morning of May 1922 (about the 22nd), he and J. Philips (since deceased) were standing on the deck of the latter's boat, anchored near the Pulteney Point lighthouse, on Malcolm Island. It was windy and the sea was rough, with waves coming in from the northwest. "We were on stand-by," Cook recalled, "keeping a look-out for the lighthouse tender when I saw the boat coming in our direction. I called to my companion that the tender was coming but did not have his sail up. We saw what we thought was the mast; but as the creature came closer we could see that it was its head and neck out of the water. We were really frightened by what we saw and breathed a sigh of relief when it kept on going — although it had a most gentle appearance and had eyes similar to those of a cow and seemed to have a film over them."

The animal swam to within 100 feet of their boat. Cook estimated its length at about 25 feet; the neck stuck out of the water seven feet and the animal appeared only about one foot wide. Cook's original sketch is reproduced as Figure 7. The creature was brown, with a "scaly appearance". Mouth and nostrils were visible and the observers were struck by its large, timid eyes. It moved at about six mph in the absence of any observable current, its head moving back and forth "like a snake". It seemed interested in its surroundings and looked gentle. [13]

Figure 7.
The animal seen by Cook and Philips off Malcolm Island in May 1922. (FROM LEBLOND AND SIBERT, 1973).

Another interesting sighting, reported later in the press but having taken place in 1925, was reported by Jack Nord, of Oyster River. Nord and his friend Peter Anderson "were returning from Cape Mudge to Menzies Bay. When abreast of Race Point," said Nord, "I happened to look to my right, and there he was, laying on top of the water." Anderson dived into the cabin for his gun and shot (and missed) twice at the animal before it submerged. "It was about thirty five yards from us," continued Nord, "and we judged it to be 100 to 110 feet long. Its body we estimated was about two and a half feet in diameter. Its head was as large as a draught horse's but it looked more like a camel's. It had fangs in its mouth six to eight inches long. Its eyes seemed to roll from a reddish to green. It had whiskers under its jaw and a kind of mane from its forehead to the back of its head looking like the teeth of a drag saw. A fin on its back reached to about three feet. From the water to the top of its head would be about seven feet. It sure was an ugly thing to see. The shooting and the bullets landing near it did not seem to bother it."[14]

Years after the fact, writer Hubert Evans revealed that in 1932, he and his friends, Dick Reeve and Bob Stephens, had seen a sea-serpent off Roberts Creek, on the Sechelt coast of the Strait of Georgia. They first saw a series of bumps appear in the water, silhouetted against the setting sun. Then, a shaft seemed to emerge until it was six or eight feet out of the water. The thought that the object might be a log was soon dismissed: "...as we stood watching, none of us breathing a word, the top end of this shaft began to elongate horizontally, until we were presented with the profile of a head, very much like a horse's in general shape, with eye bumps, nostrils, and something in the way of ears or horns. The neighbour down the way said it had stuff hanging down like hair, but I didn't see that," said Evans.[15] A camera was quickly found, but, alas!, no film.

Reports of sea-serpents in B.C. coastal waters clearly do not stop at Indian legends. Early settlers independently came across large, unidentifiable creatures which they labelled serpents or monsters, usually unaware that the natives already had names for them. Fear of ridicule and lack of scientific interest condemned many of these observations to oblivion. Soon, however, Caddy was to acquire its name and a much brighter public profile.

CHAPTER II

FRONT-PAGE NEWS!

"Any fool can disbelieve in sea serpents..."
Archie Wills, 1933

April 14, 1933, remains a memorable date in the history of crypto-zoology. On that day, Mr. and Mrs. John MacKay, tenants of the Drumnadrochit Hotel on the north shore of Loch Ness, were motoring back home from Inverness when they saw, at the northern end of the lake, a "tremendous upheaval": an enormous black body was rolling up and down at the surface of the water. By the time they had stopped the car, all that was left was ripples. A report of their sighting appeared in the May 2, 1933, issue of the *Inverness Courier*: the modern legend of the Loch Ness "Monster" was born. The London papers immediately took a keen interest in Nessie and by the autumn of that year, the story had become an international sensation.

This was certainly not the first time that large, unidentified marine animals had been spotted in lakes and oceans. Perhaps it was the mood of the time, perhaps zoological mysteries were a welcome relief from depressing news of world-wide conflict; in any case, Nessie received wide and intense coverage.

If it was fashionable for the London press to take an interest in strange water creatures, it was certainly acceptable for colonial newspapers to follow suit. When a large sea-serpent was sighted near Victoria in October 1933 it immediately became front-page

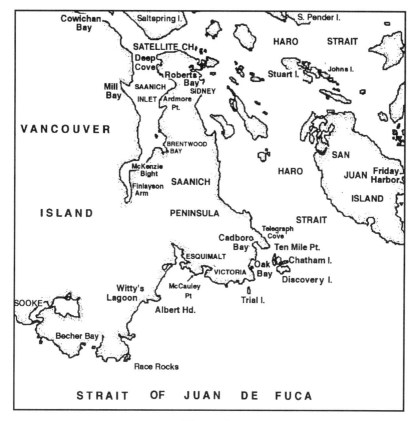

Figure 8.
The area around Victoria, where many Caddy sightings have taken place.

news. Right next to reports of the Spanish Civil War and of Japanese attacks in northern China, the *Victoria Daily Times* announced in bold letters on October 5:

"YACHTSMEN TELL OF HUGE SEA SERPENT OFF VICTORIA

Major W.H.Langley and F.W.Kemp Describe Sighting Unusual Creature. Monster Seen on Two Different Occasions; Both Descriptions Identical.

A giant sea-serpent, described as being nearly eighty feet long and about as wide as the average automobile, was seen last Sunday near Chatham Island."

The character of the witnesses, Major W.H. Langley, barrister and clerk of the provincial Legislative Assembly, and his wife, and Mr. F.W. Kemp, an employee of the Provincial Archives, and his family, spoke well for their credibility.

The Langleys had been sailing slowly and silently in their yacht *Dorothy* on a beautiful sunny day, Sunday, October 1, 1933, with a nice northerly breeze; it was about 1:30 p.m. when they heard "a very loud noise, something between a grunt and a snort accompanied by a huge hiss". They saw a "huge object, 90 to 100 feet off, a little off the port bow, and on the edge of the kelp just off the Chatham Island shore." Although they saw the creature only for a few seconds, and concluded that they had seen only a huge dome of what was apparently a portion of its back, they agreed that "it was every bit as big as the back of a large whale, but entirely different in many respects." Its colour was of greenish brown or dark olive green, with serrated markings along the top and sides. Shortly after it went down, a swirl appeared on the surface of the water ahead of the *Dorothy*. Mrs. Langley saw the animal break water a short time afterward; "the appearance was very similar, but it was much farther away and had travelled fast."

The *Daily Times* added that a previous encounter, in the very same area, had taken place a year earlier. On August 10, 1932, F.W. Kemp had been holidaying on Chatham Island with his wife and son when the incident occurred; Kemp had not told anyone of his encounter with the sea-serpent, with the exception of the agent of the Marine Department, and would probably have gone on nursing his secret if he had not met Major Langley. The Kemps had been sitting on the beach, near the northern end of the island, when Mrs. Kemp called the family's attention to a commotion in the water which threw a wash against the rocks similar to that caused by a motorboat. They saw a "mysterious something coming through the channel." In his signed statement, Mr. Kemp reports that they observed with astonishment:

"A huge creature with head out of the water travelling at four miles per hour against the tide. Even at that [low] speed a considerable wash was thrown on the rocks, which gave me the impression that it was much more reptile than serpent to make so much a displacement.

"The channel at this point is about 500 yards wide. Swimming to the steep rocks of the island opposite, the creature shot its head out of the water on to the rock, and moving its head from side to side, appeared to be taking its bearings. Then fold after fold of its body came to the surface. Towards the tail it appeared serrated, like the cutting edge of a saw, with something moving flail-like at the extreme end. The movements were like those of a crocodile. Around the head appeared a sort of mane, which drifted round the body like kelp."

The animal, perhaps disturbed by the observers, slid back into deep water. "There was a great commotion under the surface and it disappeared like a flash."

Mr. Kemp made estimates of the creature's size by measuring logs on the shore where it had beached itself briefly. The animal was considerably longer than one 60-foot log. He also put a newspaper on the spot where it had laid its head and observed it from their previous vantage point. "The animal's head was very much larger than the double sheet of newspaper. The body must have been at least 5 feet thick," he added, "and was of a bluish-green colour which shone in the sun like aluminium. I could not determine the shape of the head, but it was much thicker than the body."

Although the descriptions provided by Kemp and Langley seem to differ in many details, the latter wrote that: "Upon comparing notes with Mr. Kemp, the appearance of this object tallies with the creature that he and others saw about a year ago in the same neighbourhood."[1] The two had indeed compared notes, in the office of Archie Wills, managing editor of the *Victoria Daily Times*, who had extracted signed statements from each witness and had decided, on the basis of their character and the nature of their stories, to go ahead with publication. The definitive interpretation of the Kemp sighting, prepared by an artist for the *Times*, is seen in Figure 9, where the bulk given to the animal below the water line conforms to Kemp's impression of its displacement. Langley's description of a domed back with serrated top and edges would apply to the central part of the animal. If one is to take Kemp's statement at face value, the animal was undulating sideways, in a horizontal plane, "like a crocodile".

Wills kept the sea-serpent in the limelight for the rest of the week, soliciting signed reports from other witnesses as well as suggestions for a name for the creature. On Saturday, October 7, he warned everyone to be on the lookout for it during the

Figure 9.
*Sketch of Caddy, based on information given by Major W.H. Langley and
Mr. F.W. Kemp. (VICTORIA DAILY TIMES, 20 OCT. 1933).*

Thanksgiving long weekend. That no one saw it during the
weekend was itself taken as worthy of front-page mention: "Sea
Serpent Unreported" proclaimed the *Victoria Daily Times* on
October 10.

It soon transpired that there had been prior sightings of the
sensational creature, in Cadboro Bay in particular. Mrs. Dorothea
Hooper had reported to Wills that, about a week before Major
Langley's encounter, she had observed a similar animal cavorting
in the middle of Cadboro Bay, 400 yards away. It was about 8:30
in the morning when she saw from her house, high on the rocks
on the east side of the bay, an object which "on first appearance
resembled a gable of a house floating in the water." After she
watched it for a few minutes, Mrs. Hooper reported that "it began
to move and caused quite a commotion in the water which made
me take greater notice. As I watched, the creature began to move
slowly out to sea and its back looked much like the roof of a shed
as it sped along the top of the water."[2] While Mrs. Hooper's observation is of interest because it is associated with the naming of the
animal, it is quite poor in anatomical details: one might imagine
that the "shed roof" appearance refers to a serrated back, as
described by Mr. Kemp. At a distance of 400 yards one should
perhaps not expect anything more.

The first mention of the name Cadborosaurus appeared on
October 11, 1933: "Several suggestions for names for the monster
have been received by the Times, one of which is 'Cadborosaurus',
which can be shortened to 'Caddy' in honor of Cadboro Bay where

the creature was first sighted."[3] The original letter suggesting the name was somewhat tongue-in-cheek; the signer, I. Vacedun, could not be traced; his address seemed to be that of a well-known local jail, and Wills suspected that the letter might have originated from a reporter on a rival newspaper, the *Daily Colonist.*

"The News Editor of
The Victoria Daily Times

Dear Sir,

Why not Cadborosaurus as a name for our new sea pet? It's only fair that the locality from which he was most often sighted and Possibly first discovered, should get the credit from Posterity when he may have retired to the limbo of other monsters of land and sea. Besides the name is euphonious, and, if too long, can be shortened to "Caddy" as a pet name, especially for the lucky ones who see him from the nineteenth hole at Oak Bay.

Yours truly,

I. Vacedun
Wilkinson Road, Saanich

Oct. 6 /33

British Columbians! Lift up a chorus!
To greet the arrival of Cadborosaurus!
He may have been here quite a long time before us,
But he's shy and don't stay round too long, so's to bore us.
Cadborosaurus! Cadborosaurus!
Come up and see us again, you old war 'oss!"[4]

There was intense rivalry at the time between the *Times* and its senior competitor, the *Colonist.* The latter was at first rather cool to the whole idea of a sea-serpent. It had reported the Kemp and Langley sightings, a day after the *Times*, but on the whole, it seemed to consider the affair a publicity stunt. While the *Times* featured the novelty creature day after day, the *Colonist* mentioned the sea-serpent only disparagingly, publishing (on October 12) a picture of dolphins stranded on a California beach and (on October 14) a suggestion that it might be a conger eel. On October 15, the *Colonist* could not resist scooping its rival with a new sighting, by Charles F. Eagles, also in Cadboro Bay, on October 14. Eagles copyrighted his Caddy sketch and sold it as a postcard (Figure 10). The *Colonist* went on to propose its own name, Amy, for the sea-serpent, without ever mentioning Cadborosaurus or Caddy.[5] Both names were in use for a brief time, but Caddy quickly won out. Even the *Colonist* soon began to speak of "Amy Cadborosaurus".

Except for a short hiatus around Sunday, October 15, perhaps not to alarm the participants of an attempt to swim across Juan de Fuca Strait, Archie Wills kept Caddy continuously in the news and brought forth more testimonies of its existence. Some of these dated from earlier years and have been mentioned above. Others were more current. Mr. and Mrs. R.H. Bryden reported seeing Caddy near Trial Island "a week after Major Langley".

Figure 10.
The first Caddy postcard, sketched from life by Charles F. Eagles, on 14 Oct. 1933. Body approximate length 20 feet, diameter eight feet, tail 30 feet, head and neck ten feet. Total length 60 feet.

Figure 11.
Caddy's "godfather", Archie H. Wills. (PHOTOGRAPH PROVIDED BY MR. K. WILLS).

"I was rowing home after fishing off Trial Island and was heading towards Oak Bay," said Mr. Bryden, "when I heard a great commotion in the water to my right, between the boat and the shore." After his wife suddenly shouted: "Goodness, Bert, what is that?" Bryden said that he looked over his right shoulder and "distinctly saw two curved sections of the monster, which was spouting water with a gushing sound. The two humps I saw were separated by many feet of water. As I looked the monster, which appeared to be of a dark green color, disappeared beneath the surface. I was so near it that I had to stop rowing to avoid colliding with it. My first reaction was that the monster we had seen was a whale but on further reflection and on hearing the stories about the sea serpent I concluded that it could not have been a whale."[6] Both Bryden and his wife mentioned the "serrated back" of the animal, which resembled the sketch of Caddy already published in the *Times* (Figure 9).

That same year, on October 21, at the end of a long journey from New York, the master of the Grace liner *Santa Lucia*, Captain Walter Prengel, and his navigating officer, J. Richardson, saw a strange object in the water in the early morning mists, a few miles from Victoria Harbour. They had decided not to mention their "apparition", but discovering that everyone in Victoria was talking about Caddy, Captain Prengel related how "My navigating officer called my attention to a big, peculiarly-shaped object about 300 feet away. At first we decided it was an upturned barge, but on further observations, we saw it moving, and moving rapidly too. It was in sight only a minute or two," Captain Prengel continued, "before it dived beneath the surface. We could only see what was probably the head of the serpent, and it looked from the bridge of the ship to be about the size of my cabin. We could see none of the after portions at all. It was rather misty at the time. It cut quite a wake, and when it disappeared it left a wide area of foam, as if a giant tail had lashed the water." Prengel added that "the head seemed to be light brown in color, with white streaks running up and down it."[7]

Speculation as to the nature of the animal arose immediately. An editorial of October 7, 1933, presumably written by Wills, proclaimed that: "There is abundant unimpeachable evidence that some strange marine monster either has its home in the Gulf of Georgia or frequently visits those waters. The detailed reports of responsible citizens of what they have seen of the stranger and its activities transfer it from the world of fiction to that of reality."

The concluding paragraph brought up explanations current at the time: "It is believed by some that the thing belongs to the giant squid family, known to frequent the coasts of Newfoundland, Scandinavia and the British Isles. Others contend that it is a plesiosaurus, a huge marine reptile which was thought to have been extinct. Captain Hope, of H.M.S. *Fly*, reported that he had seen in the Gulf of California a monster with the body of an alligator. Whatever the mammal may be — huge squid or plesiosaurus, — it certainly has been seen in the Gulf, and its presence reminds us that there still are more things in heaven and earth — and the sea as well — that are not dreamed of in the little two-by-four philosophy of mankind."[8]

News of the British Columbia sea-serpent excited world-wide interest and put Victoria "on the map", to the great delight of the local Chamber of Commerce, which would become Caddy's staunchest supporter. The *New York Herald Tribune* announced the sea-serpent's existence on October 6, the day following publication of the Langley and Kemp sightings and regularly kept its readers informed of further progress. Even *The Vancouver Sun* had to admit: "Whole Continent Intrigued by Caddy's Capers."[9]

Comments, suggestions, support, and ridicule rained in from everywhere. A San Diego businessman, George P. Wilson, wrote to the Victoria Chamber of Commerce with specific instructions on how to catch Caddy, based on his experience in catching large sharks and manta rays: "the hook should be at least one foot long and six inches wide..."[10] Seattle fishermen ventured to suggest that "Old Hiaschuckoluk, [a variant of *hiyitl'iik*] was nothing but a giant conger eel", generating a flurry of denials.[11] "The creature we saw off Chatham Island is no more a conger eel than my hat," replied F.W. Kemp.[12] Newspaper columns were inundated by suggestions about what Caddy might be: an elephant seal, a ribbon fish, a whale. People took an interest in marine zoology and newspapers sold.

Scientific opinion was also sought. Francis Kermode, director of the Provincial Museum, expressed a "lively interest in marine apparitions".[13] The province's most eminent zoologist, Dr. C. McLean Fraser, F.R.S.C., Head of the Zoology Department at the University of British Columbia, expressed the view that "Until someone gets a lasso around one of these things we will never be able to get much farther. It is possible that there are such things."[14] He also ventured to speculate that the sea-serpent might be a survivor of the Mesozoic age of dinosaurs, a possibility which Wills called upon when explaining the choice of the name Cadborosaurus as fitting in "with the designations by which other prehistoric animals are known."[15] Another zoological authority, Professor Trevor Kincaid, of the University of Washington, was quoted as saying: "It seems strange that if such creatures do exist, one wouldn't have been captured by this time. Still, all accounts seem to tally. And that might mean something."[16] The absence of a specimen presented a major obstacle to definite scientific recognition.

After two weeks of intense discussion of older and recent sightings, what emerged was a view of Caddy as a real animal, shown in Figure 12, where the artist embodied "the various features described by many eyewitnesses into one sea serpent"[17]: the first of many attempts to synthesize the animal from disparate observations. The creature depicted has a long, serpentine body, apparently undulating in the vertical plane; much importance is

Figure 12.
A first synthesis of Caddy observations, presented in the VICTORIA DAILY TIMES, 21 Oct. 1933.

placed on the serrations along its back; the head resembles that of a horse, with ears and mane.

From spectacular beginnings in October 1933, Caddy has remained front-page news in the Victoria press to this day and has entered the marine folklore of local waters. As an astute editor, Archie Wills was well aware of the publicity value of Caddy, pointing out quickly that the "realization grows that Victoria has something which will bring it fame incomparably faster than the population, trade and crime figures of Vancouver."[18] Looking deeper, he noted with disappointment the cynicism of his fellow citizens. "Your modern man would rather disbelieve something than believe it," he wrote. "He likes to think he is cynical and hard-boiled, whereas he is the most credulous creature ever made. When he can't understand a thing, like astronomy, or relativity, or finance, he believes anything you care to tell him, if you tell him with sufficient scientific or financial trimmings. But the trouble is he can understand a sea serpent. He can visualize it. Therefore, he disbelieves it. His disbelief flatters his vanity, makes him think he is a superior fellow. Well, it doesn't make him a superior fellow. Any fool can disbelieve in sea serpents...."[19]

The evidence so strongly brought forward by Wills in the 1930s forced the press, the public and even the scientists to consider seriously the possibility that there was perhaps a real animal, a "cryptid", to be discovered some day and brought to the fold of established zoology.

Wills spread the word about Caddy widely, in other Canadian papers and in Europe.[20] To the end of his days, he felt proud and possessive about "his sea-serpent". In a letter in 1970, he wrote: "I introduced Caddy to the world in 1933 and have enjoyed being his sponsor and protector."[21] If anyone is to be credited with discovering Caddy and perhaps to be honoured by having his name linked to its official description, it should be A.H. "Archie" Wills. *Cadborosaurus willsi*, has been proposed as Caddy's official scientific name.[22]

CHAPTER III

A CONTINUING PRESENCE

Following its official recognition and baptism in October 1933, Caddy continued to be featured regularly in coastal British Columbia newspapers. The list of sightings presented in Appendix I, although perhaps not exhaustive, gives a good idea of the regularity of its appearances over the past century; Figure 13 shows the distribution of reported sightings by decade; most of those mentioned in the text occurred within the area depicted in Figure 14. Although sightings peaked in the 1930s and 1940s, perhaps because of the publicity which it received at that time, Caddy continues to be observed with some regularity to this day. The "Caddy phenomenon" was clearly more than just a passing fad, created by an imaginative editor to boost circulation.

While the sightings publicized by Archie Wills mostly took place in the vicinity of Victoria, it quickly became clear that Caddy, or at least something very much like it, had been seen and continued to be seen in many other locations. The protected waters of the Strait of Georgia and eastern Juan de Fuca Strait have yielded by far the greatest number of sightings, but there are also reports from the outer coast, from California up to Alaska.

The prototype Caddy described in previous chapters is a large, serpentine animal characterized by a serrated back and a horse-like head. Additional observations soon brought in more details as well as puzzling variations, as a review of the most striking sightings shows.

Caddy was still a novelty item when, on an early Sunday
morning in December 1933, Cyril Andrews and his younger friend
Norman Georgeson went out duck hunting off Gowlland Head,
near their home on South Pender Island. "I succeeded in shooting
a 'golden eye' duck," said Andrews, "but as I had only broken its

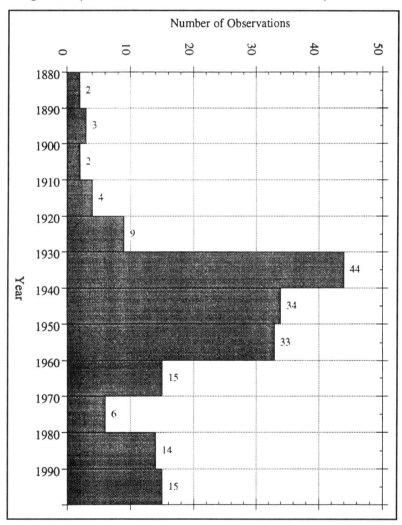

Figure 13.
Frequency of Caddy sightings included in Appendix I, by decade.

wing, it began to swim to a kelp bed about fifty yards from shore.
Seeing that I could not get the wounded bird I sent Norman home
for a small punt, five feet long. Returning, he was paddling across
the bay towards me as I walked over a little rise to see if he was
coming. As I looked across the water I saw a head disappear some
distance out. From where I was standing I could plainly see the
whole body of a sea monster just moving a foot underneath the
surface.

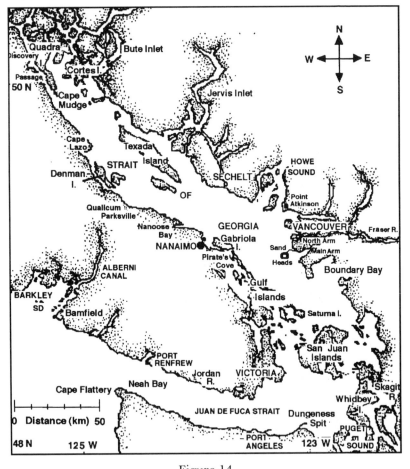

Figure 14.
*Southern British Columbia waters, with locations of Caddy sightings mentioned in
the text. For reports near Victoria, see Figure 8.*

"Thinking I might alarm Norman," Andrews continued, "I did not draw his attention to what I saw, so he came along and picked me up at the point from which we had shot the bird. From there we paddled to the wounded bird in the kelp bed. I was sitting in the front of the punt ready to pick up the bird, when about ten feet away, out of the sea rose two coils. They reached a height of at least six feet above me, gradually sinking under the water again, when a head appeared. The head was that of a horse, without ears or nostrils, but its eyes were in front of its head, which was flat just like a horse.

"I attracted Georgeson's attention to it and he saw one coil and the head well clear of the water. Then the whole thing except the head, which remained just out of the water, sank. I was still only ten feet away from it, with the duck right beside the thing, when to my horror it gulped the bird down its throat. It then looked at me, its mouth wide open, and I could plainly see its teeth and tongue, which were like those of a fish. I would swear to the head being three feet long and two feet wide. When it closed its mouth, all the loose skin folded in neatly at the corners while its breathing came in short, sharp pants, like a dog after a run.

"At that point," continued Andrews, "a number of sea gulls swooped down at the creature, which snapped at them when they came too close. Shortly after this it sank below the surface."[1] The two young men called in Justice of the Peace G.F. Parkyn, who took down an affidavit of what they had seen. By that time (about ten minutes later), the creature surfaced again 20 yards from

Figure 15.
Cyril Andrews and Norman Georgeson meet Caddy at South Pender Island. (From *Archie Wills' scrapbook*).

Figure 16.
Sketches of Caddy by Cyril Andrews. (FROM ARCHIE WILLS' SCRAPBOOK).

shore, swimming away in an undulating motion. Eleven other people also saw it, including Mr. Parkyn.

The head of the creature resembled that of a horse, without ears, nostrils or whiskers. The tongue came to a point and its teeth were fish-like. In colour it was a gray-brown with a dark brown stripe running along the body slightly to one side (Figure 16). The animal was two feet in diameter; no fins or flippers were seen. Five humps protruded above the water surface, but there was no indication of any serration on its back. The absence of this feature suggested a slightly different animal than that seen by Kemp and Langley. Popular speculation suggested that "Penda" Cadborosaurus, as it was soon called, might be a female of the species. No firm biological support for this interpretation was ever brought forward. Nevertheless, the Caddy family was growing.

Andrews and his friends, Arthur Pender and Kathleen Georgeson, saw Caddy again on December 21, in Plumper Sound; a third time, on January 18, 1934, Andrews and Pender, this time accompanied by Eileen McKay, watched the animal near Bedwell Harbour, South Pender Island. "We could plainly see it undulating, as it travelled towards Wallace Point. Apparently it was feeding time, because it went out to the herring bed, and

Figure 17.
Cyril Andrews (left) and friends Kathleen Georgeson and Arthur Pender. (FROM VICTORIA DAILY TIMES, *23 JAN. 1934*).

there we watched it for twenty-five minutes. There were sea gulls flying around it and they kept pecking at it. 'Penda' snapped at them, but did not get any that we saw." Andrews confirmed that this was the same animal he had seen on previous occasions, with a "dark stripe along its back, and not a sign of flippers or fins. Another thing we could see was that it had a flesh coloured face with no whiskers."[2]

It was also thought to be "Penda" Cadborosaurus that was seen during that same period by Coronel Marsh, Earl Marsh and J.W. Chilton near Trial Island. The three eyewitnesses saw the "female" Caddy reaching for a sea gull, which it devoured.[3]

Another man who had quite a close look at Caddy was a naval officer from the Canadian Navy base at Esquimalt. While the *Victoria Daily Times* knew the officer's name, the newspaper agreed to withhold it, calling him only "Lieutenant Commander X". On a sunny afternoon in November 1950, he was fishing from an open boat, about a third of a mile off Esquimalt Harbour, between McCauley and Brothers islands. There was a heavy swell and a stiff breeze, but visibility was excellent. The lure was about 70 feet out and Caddy crossed astern, inside the lure. "He was 30 feet from head to tail and created a heavy wash," said the officer. "He surfaced about every 35 feet. Each time he lifted his head from the water he opened his mouth wide and showed two rows of large teeth which had a saw-tooth appearance. Before he dove he snapped his teeth together with a terrifying sound."

The officer said Caddy's head was something like that of an ordinary garden snake. It was about 18 inches across and two feet in length. The eyes, jet black, were between two and three inches in diameter. Caddy's head sat on a neck about six feet long and, where it joined the body, there seemed to be shoulders. It propelled itself with large flippers on either side and its enormous tail appeared flat like that of a beaver. Caddy's body had a gradual hump but in no part was it serrated. He observed no gills in the head. The head and body were covered with hair, brown in colour. For 25 seconds, Lieutenant Commander X had a good look at Caddy. "I don't mind admitting that I was terrified," he concluded, "especially when it snapped its jaws."[4]

Most of the observations describe a creature with a head resembling that of a horse, a camel or a giraffe. Rarely is there specific mention of the absence of ears: this was stated, for example by Cyril Andrews, who had a very close look, and by two women who saw an animal with a "head like a horse except it had no ears..." off Sechelt in September 1947.[5] More frequently, however, there is express reference to something on the head: ears or horns.

One who definitely saw horns was Roy Duesenbury of Blakeley Island (near Pender Island) who was working on his wood pile at

Figure 18.
An encounter with Caddy. (FROM ARCHIE WILLS' SCRAPBOOK).

mid-morning in November 1940, when he heard a sound like a rush of wind. "The monstrosity had a head like a horse with two horns, which were blunt."[6] The neck appeared to be short, but the whole animal was about 40 feet long.

Ian Sherwin and Herbert Winship also had a good look at Caddy in McKenzie Bight, Saanich Inlet, in January 1954. The animal was moving slowly along the shore, showing the top of coils behind it as shown in Figure 19. The motion was clearly up and down and when it finally submerged, it went down snout first. The eyes were set to look forward and "behind the eye there was a bulge that gave the appearance of an ear." Concluding the letter in which he describes the incident, Sherwin states his views as to the value of publicizing the sighting: "Since I was starting out in my own timber business I was not at the time in a hurry to be known as a person who saw sea serpents."[7] This is a reaction typical of many eyewitnesses.

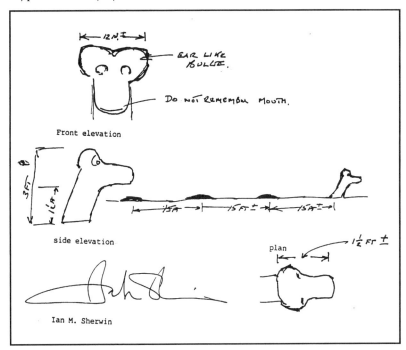

Figure 19.
Caddy, as sketched by Ian Sherwin.

N. Erickson, a fisherman from Sointula, B.C., was sure that he saw ears. Erickson was travelling about one mile west of the Merry Island lighthouse, in the Strait of Georgia, on July 7, 1957. The sea was calm, the weather clear; it was about eight p.m. and the sun was low on the horizon. "I noticed this object that I thought was a three-foot driftwood," he wrote, "but getting closer, I noticed splashing at one end which I thought was a duck trying to climb onto it. Getting closer then I noticed big nostrils at the other end and the splashing was that it was flipping his ears. It was only the head on the surface. When I got as close as 20 yards, it just submerged and disappeared. After I ran over him, he came to the surface just 15 feet behind the boat. I could see two humps on his back, but the sun was setting behind it so that I could not see what kind of a back end he had, nor for sure how long it was. What I saw was 12 -15 ft long."[8]

The animal, sketched in Figure 20, was brown, 12 or more feet long and four feet wide; it had no mane, in spite of its equine appearance, but very short brown fur. Ears, eyes, mouth and

Figure 20.
Caddy, as seen by fisherman N. Erickson: a. first sight, head on surface; b. second sight, with more body emerging. (FROM LEBLOND AND SIBERT, 1973).

nostrils were clearly visible. It remained at the surface after Erickson's passage until he couldn't see it in the distance.

The confusion between ears and horns stands out clearly in a remarkable sighting which occurred on the coast of Oregon, just after New Year's Day, 1937, about two miles south of Yachats, and about a dozen miles north of the famous sea-lion caves. At that point, just south of Cape Perpetua, there is a chasm in the rocky shoreline known as the Devil's Churn. The weather was stormy, with rain and wind and a very rough sea. Bill Hunt and his wife were sitting on a landing, about 30 feet above sea level, along the switchback trail which leads from the parking area near the highway to the Churn, watching the spectacular breakers.

They first sighted the creature about 200 feet seaward of the mouth of the Churn. It was coming directly towards shore, swimming slowly without visible propelling motions. It then stopped close to the entrance of the chasm (only about 100 feet away from the Hunts), where the heavy breakers did not seem to toss it around one bit. A truck came by on the highway at that time; the animal turned its head to look at it, then looked at the observers, then back at the truck. It then took off southwards along the coast, at a speed of about 25 knots. The Hunts followed on the highway in their car. At an observation point about a mile south of the Churn, the animal was about 300 feet offshore. It then veered off the coast seawards. An unidentified man stopped his car at the lookout and they all watched the creature swim out to sea until they could see it no more.

In addition to the sketch shown in Figure 21, the Hunts noted that the animal had a long neck ("at least 15 feet"), and a head which reminded them variously of a horse, a giraffe or a camel. A mane the colour of seaweed (on Pacific shores the most prominent seaweeds are brown algae) was visible on the neck all the way down to the body. The body itself was about six feet across, with a ridge running along the top. Hunt said that when the animal was in a trough, he noticed a tail, which was as long as the body itself, giving a total length of about 55 feet. While Hunt noticed small ears which "fluttered incessantly", his wife thought that the animal had small, straight horns on its head, eight to ten inches high and "the size of a small water-pipe."[9]

Similar confusion about the nature of head appendages was expressed by R.D. Cockburn, C.P. Crawford and Ron Loach in

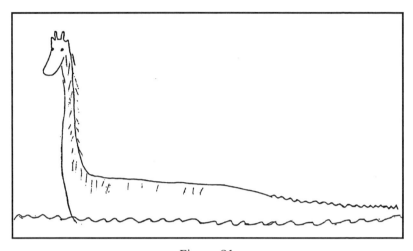

Figure 21.
The Yachats sea-serpent. (FROM LEBLOND AND SIBERT, 1973).

describing the animal which they saw off Qualicum Beach in 1953. To quote Cockburn: "At first I doubted what I saw. I could see a head and three bumps, but I thought it must be three or four seals cavorting about. But then the thing reared up a few feet out of the water and I could see it was just one animal. We watched for a good five minutes. Two other men put out in a row boat towards it. When they got within 15-20 feet, it submerged and reappeared 100 yards away. It had the general shape of a snake with three distinctive humps, an equal distance apart, and a dog-shaped head with two protusions, possibly horns."[10] Cockburn added that when the creature reared up, its head and neck looked something like a giraffe's.

Only one description mentions both ears and horns. On a bright sunny morning in January 1984, mechanical engineer Jim N. Thompson was fishing for salmon off Spanish Banks (Vancouver) in his motorized Folbot kayak. He was approximately 200 yards north of the most westerly Spanish Banks channel marker; the sea was calm, apart from a moderate swell. Glancing south towards the mouth of the Fraser River he saw for five to ten seconds a furry, somewhat serpent-like creature, approximately 100 feet away. "It surfaced in the trough of a swell and looked back at me," he wrote, "while moving westward quite fast. It appeared to be 18'-20' long with a craned neck and a smallish camel or giraffe-like head pointed in my direction. I discounted its being a sea otter swimming on its back. Definitely furry — at the head end anyway — and was gliding in an up-and-down swimming motion at an estimated 15-20 mph. It submerged into a crest and I did not see it again. I never mentioned it to anyone before — not even to my wife who may have poo-pooed it anyway. It was 22-26" wide; 4 ft emerged out of the water. It was whitish tan in colour on the throat & lower front to a solid tan upper head. It had small horns: giraffe-type stubs; and what appeared to be large, floppy ears, with one bent forward over the forehead. Eyes and mouth were clearly visible."[11] Thompson's original sketch is shown in Figure 22.

Vancouver restaurateur Peter Pantages, his wife Helen, and a friend, Chris Altman, also saw Caddy when fishing in English Bay, somewhere between the bell buoy and Siwash Rock, in 1947. According to Mrs. Pantages, the animal had a horse's face and three humps. It swam up and down like a caterpillar. Its skin was dark, but not as dark as that of a "blackfish" (a pilot whale). Both Mrs. Pantages and Mr. Altman noticed the large eyes; they also heard the animal snort as it blew water through its nose. [12]

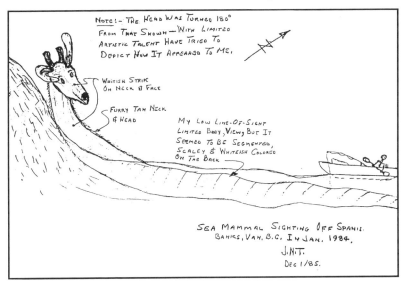

Figure 22.
Jim Thompson's sketch of Caddy off Spanish Banks, Vancouver.

Other descriptions of Caddy have been offered. To the boys who said they saw Caddy in the Fraser River (at the foot of Main Street, Vancouver) in January 1934, it had a head like that of a cow, with horns or ears, mounted on a four-foot neck.[13] To T. Liston, fishing for cod in the Strait of Georgia in the summer of 1941, who said that he got "a real good look at him and he got a good look at me too", when it swam within 15 feet of his boat, its head was "shaped like a seal's but with a much longer neck."[14] The animal he saw was 20 feet long, six or seven inches in diameter at its thickest part, with a two-foot fin on its back. To W. Kennedy, the animal which he saw off his waterfront property in West Vancouver, at the mouth of Howe Sound, had a head which was serpentine in character, approximately 18 inches in length and 12 inches in cross section, without ears or horns.[15] He and the animal watched each other at a distance of 30 feet for about three minutes. The creature was grey-brown and smooth-haired, like a seal. About 3 1/2 feet of neck and head emerged from the water at an angle of 45°.

A number of reports mention a mane (the Hunts) or body hair (Kennedy). A mane was also mentioned by a Vancouver couple, Mr. and Mrs. Didsbury, who saw "a creature with a long neck which seemed to have a sort of mane near the head" near shore off Finlayson Point, Victoria, in December 1950.[16] John McIntyre, a visitor from Los Angeles, took a picture of an animal in Brentwood Bay, Saanich Inlet, "brownish in colour with a sort of dirty hair covering the long neck. The head was rather like that of a camel with large eyes."[17] Unfortunately, Mr. McIntyre dropped his camera in the water in the excitement of the moment. The animal which Ron Winkelman saw in Stuart Channel in 1946, and which he described as horse-headed, with ears, large round eyes, and brown-grey in colour, also had a mane.[18]

A close encounter, about half a mile southeast of the Discovery Island light, involved fisherman David Miller of Victoria. In his own words: "While engaged in commercial fishing one afternoon in late November 1959, my partner Alfred Webb and I observed this strange creature surface roughly 80 feet on our port beam. It started to move rapidly away from us so we speeded the engine up and gave chase. We got within 30 feet when it suddenly submerged, not in the method of seals or sea-lions but as though something pulled it under. A few moments later we arrived at its place of submergence and there was a tremendous turbulence, suggesting a creature the size of a 30-foot sei whale. Its speed under water was also astounding as it surfaced a few minutes later over a hundred yards away. It stayed up while we took off after it again but this time it never let us get close again." Miller provided the sketch shown in Figure 23. He and Webb clearly noted the large red eyes and short ears, visible at the short range when the creature was first seen. Miller added that "other fishermen friends have also reported strange creatures much resembling the one we saw but are reluctant to report it to the papers or authorities because of the usual ridicule which follows such sightings."[19]

Other features are sometimes mentioned: in the following case, prominent lips. In December 1962, Mrs. Robert Guy, of Lantzville, near Nanaimo, and her friend Mrs. K.B. Holland watched through binoculars from the former's living room a strange animal, about 200 yards away near some pilings. Its head was like a camel's and dark brown in colour. Its mouth appeared to have "the exaggerated lips one sees in a minstrel show."[20] A large hump came out of the water behind the head; the animal swam with an undulating motion.

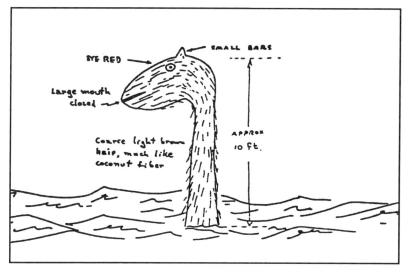

Figure 23.
The animal seen by David Miller and Alfred Webb near Discovery Island. (FROM LEBLOND AND SIBERT, 1973).

Caddy is vocal. A number of witnesses have mentioned hearing sounds associated with their sighting. For example, Arthur P. Dawe had a good look at Caddy through binoculars from his home on Cadboro Bay. "It had something of a camel's head and three distinct undulations. It would dive and then come to the surface and 'blow'. When I heard the blow, I thought it might be a blackfish, and I studied it closer, but it was no blackfish and it wasn't a porpoise or a sea lion. It seemed to be feeding and stayed off our place for five minutes. Then it dove and disappeared."[21]

Caddy has been reported eating fish, but it also has a weakness for birds. The animal Cyril Andrews encountered ate the duck he had just shot; there was also the account of "Penda" leaping at a sea gull. Another incident involving birds was observed by May Williams on an early September morning when she was awakened by a great commotion on the waters of Saanich Inlet. What she saw from her window was a giant, dark, snake-like creature battling with a large number of black ducks. The encounter lasted for about 15 minutes. The animal had a head like that of a giant snake, which it raised four or five feet above the water; coils five to six feet long, about ten feet apart, followed behind.[22]

On a similar occasion, in March 1961, Mrs. A.R. Stacey opened the blinds of her waterfront living room, in Sidney, and saw a strange animal out in the water. She followed its movements through her binoculars. At first she assumed it was a log, but she then noticed that it drifted against the tide. While watching closely she saw a head rise from the water to assume a different position, when a sea gull settled on the long neck. She took her attention away from the neck to see the end of the tail. When she glanced again at the neck, the bird had gone and the creature was looking backwards. There was no sign of the sea gull in the water or the air and she assumed that it had been eaten.[23]

There is also a graceful silhouette sketch (Figure 24) of Caddy lunging at gulls, by the hand of artist and photographer Wilfred Gibson, who saw it from his home in Mill Bay in 1943.[24]

Caddy is a very fast swimmer. Many witnesses have expressed their amazement at its speed. A striking demonstration of Caddy's abilities in this respect involves two individuals seen simultaneously in Saanich Inlet in the summer of 1993.

Pilots James Wells and Don Berends of Cooper Air Services were practising water landings in Brentwood Bay when they

Figure 24.
Caddy snatching at birds: sketched by Wilfred Gibson. (FROM ARCHIE WILLS' SCRAPBOOK).

spotted what appeared to be two large fish or seals just ahead as they landed. On taxiing closer they noted that both creatures were larger than fish or seals; each had two shallow, vertical humps, or coils, in tandem above the surface under which they could see about six inches of daylight. Each hump was three to four feet in length, one foot to 16 inches thick; the humps were about five to eight feet apart, in tandem for a total length of 12 to 14 feet from the beginning of the first hump to the end of the second. The pilots did not see a head or a tail in either animal. They could not catch up with them at taxiing speeds of up to 40 mph.[25]

Thus, there is more than one Caddy. There have been other multiple sightings. In December 1938, the crew of the tugboat *Catala Chief*, William Y. Higgs, George R. Macfarlane and John Shaw, saw two Caddies in Stuart Channel, 20 miles south of Nanaimo. The larger one was seen first; it was over 40 feet long and snake-like, with a round body. Another one about half the size then joined it.[26] An offspring? Or perhaps a mate?

The following year, another threesome, Bob Gaetz, Frank Marshall and Bill Smith, working on a telephone-company submarine-cable gang, observed a pair of Caddies cavort for 20 minutes in Satellite Channel. The larger one was quite big: about 15 feet of its body stuck out of the water in two humps and its total length was estimated at 40 feet. Its head was as big as a horse's and shaped about the same although it had no ears. It was chestnut brown, with hair on the head and body, but no fins as far as could be seen. It snorted a couple of times, and then bellowed like a cow. When it opened its mouth they could see teeth two inches long. The other one was exactly the same with a head half the size.[27]

There are even reports of Caddy being observed on land. In 1936, E.J. Stephenson, with his wife and son, observed a 90-foot-long, three-foot-thick animal wriggling over the reef into a lagoon on Saturna Island. The animal was yellow and bluish in colour.[28] More recently, in June 1991, Sidney resident Terry Osland was walking her dog, Lady, down trails to the beach near Ardmore Point, Saanich Inlet. Lady was pulling at her leash, not wanting to go down to the beach when they turned by a cliff. Then, as Mrs. Osland explained to Patrick Murphy of the *Times-Colonist*:

"I saw this face looking at me, then it disappeared over the edge and the dog was fighting to get away.

"I heard a splash and I looked over and saw the back end go into the water. It then came up twice and I saw the top of its head.

"It was bigger than a killer whale, I've seen them, and it couldn't have been an elephant seal. It was hard to describe.

"It was smooth, it had no hair and the tail was rounded like a lizard tail and it had like little feet on the side back of the tail.

"It had grey, silvery color skin that resembled the smooth skin of a dog fish. I never saw a long neck."[29]

Mrs. Osland and her dog beat a hasty and silent retreat; so did the animal, slithering down the ten-foot cliff across the beach into the water, leaving a scrape mark on the beach and a strong, rotten smell. She viewed it for about a minute from the top of the cliff before it swam away. The absence of a long neck and the presence of small hind legs are features more reminiscent of the picture of *hiyitl'iik* seen in Figure 2 than of the standard Caddy depictions.

Finally, it is significant that Caddy sightings are not just old stories; they continue to occur with some regularity. John Celona and his daughter Marjie saw Caddy in Cadboro Bay in May 1992. Marjie described it as an "extremely large, dark brown, almost black sea creature moving at low speed".[30] Doris Sinclair, of Seattle, saw it while at her vacation home in Ocean Shores, Gray's Harbor, Washington, also in 1992. "The long slender neck rose, I would say, five or six feet in the air, and the thing that struck me was that incredible dignity!" Mrs. Sinclair told author Jessica Maxwell. "The animal wasn't afraid, and each time it rose out of the water its head did a sort of ritualistic nod before it would curl down again....Every 100 feet or so it would rise, make a ritualistic forward nodding motion then arch back down into the water. It did that four or five times before I couldn't see it anymore."[31]

So Caddy is sometimes seen with a serrated back, sometimes without; it is long and snake-like, but sometimes seems to have a central body swelling; it has a horse-like head (most of the time), with big eyes; sometimes ears or horns are mentioned; a mane is often seen and body hair (seal like) is commonly mentioned; fins or flippers are rarely mentioned. There are big and small Caddies and they have been seen together. Caddy interacts with, and occasionally eats birds; it makes breathing noises and has been heard to bellow like a cow. Finally, there are observations which do not fit with this picture, which suggest the possibility of a second kind of creature.

What is this animal? How can it look so different from time to time? Are males and females different enough to account for the variability in observed features? Are the differences only apparent, and due to a lack of familiar reference points and confusion on the part of witnesses? Or is there perhaps more than one kind of Caddy? Some of Caddy's behaviour seems very realistic, but why isn't it seen more often? Has anyone ever caught a Caddy?

CHAPTER IV

ON THE BEACH

Communicated information is never as convincing as shared experience. Eyewitness reports never fully satisfy scientists who, in their systematic skepticism, insist that they must be shown or be able to touch the evidence. If Caddy exists, they have rightly insisted, show it to us; if a live specimen cannot be found, a dead one will do.

Over the years, a number of carcasses found on beaches have attracted attention and offered prospects of material evidence to satisfy the skeptics. The earliest case on record is that of a 27-foot creature found near Valdez, Alaska, on November 10, 1930. The carcass was first seen embedded in floating glacier ice by Jerry O'Leary and Charles Gibson, 1,500 feet from shore in Eagle Harbor, Glacier Island, off the former's fox farm. They towed it ashore and then to the fox-farm headquarters on the island. There, flesh was stripped off the animal and hung in a smoke house to dry for fox feed. As soon as news of the mysterious carcass reached Juneau, W.J. McDonald, Supervisor of the Chugach National Forest, was dispatched to examine and, if possible, identify the remains.

"The following measurements were announced: Head - 55 inches long, 36 inches wide; Body proper - 74 inches at widest place; Tail - 14 ft long; Skeleton - entire length more than 24 ft; estimated weight 1,000 pounds. The animal had flippers

40 inches long on each side behind the head, each with five fingers. There are seven ribs on each side. The head and tail were bare of flesh, while six feet of the mid-section was covered with meat which in texture resembled horse flesh. It had a snout similar to that of a pelican, the head is shaped similar to an elephant's. The beast apparently was toothless."[1]

Caddy had not made its public appearance at that time and there was no connection made then, or later, between the Glacier Island carcass and the sea-serpent of more southerly waters. Tentative identification at the time, suggested by Bernard Brown, curator at the American Museum of Natural History, was that it was a marine creature, perhaps one of the smaller whales, "perhaps one as yet unclassified and unknown to science."[2] The stomach and a large piece of flesh were brought back to Cordova by Mr. McDonald to be frozen and preserved for future scientific examination. It is not known whether this unidentified creature has any connection to Caddy.

In 1934, the badly decomposed remains of a 30-foot-long creature were found by fisherman Hugo Sandstrom on Henry Island, off the north end of Porcher Island, near Prince Rupert. Dr. Neal Carter, Director of the Dominion Fisheries Experimental Station in Prince Rupert, went to investigate in the fisheries patrol boat, and found the remains lying on the beach, just below the high-water mark. "The creature was possibly thirty feet long when alive," Carter said. "Some of the tail appears to be missing. I believe it had been there for some six weeks or two months because of the advanced state of decomposition. The skin resembles sand-paper, rougher than that of dogfish or shark. The upper part was covered with hair, the lower part with spines." Except for the backbone, Carter found no other bones, such as ribs, in the creature's body. Flesh which still clung to the backbone was red, similar to beef in appearance which, according to Carter, "put the creature out of the fish class." There was some evidence for fins, or flipper-like projections of cartilaginous material, about four feet long; the head was also described as cartilaginous, "like that of a calf."[3]

From the initial description of the Henry Island carcass the find was heralded as "possible proof of existence of Caddy." The *New York Herald Tribune* featured a front-page headline: "Remains of

Hairy Sea-Serpent Silence Skeptics, Baffle Scientists", linking the remains directly with "Hiaschuckaluck cadborosaurus."[4] Professor Trevor Kincaid, of the University of Washington, expressed the opinion that the creature was something previously unknown in animal life. "If it was 30 feet long," he said, "it wasn't a sea lion, or a walrus, and if it had hair and quills, it wasn't a whale."[5]

The remains were then carried back to Prince Rupert for closer examination, put on public display and photographed from every angle. Pieces of the carcass were sent to experts for identification. Mr. Francis Kermode, Director of the Provincial Museum in Victoria, offered the suggestion that the animal might be the last survivor of Steller's sea cow, extinct since the late 18th century.[6] It was proposed to purchase the carcass for display at the museum, an idea reputed to have enjoyed the favour of Premier Patullo. After having examined several portions of the hide and half a dozen hooked quills, Kermode said that he had never seen anything like this before, and that: "It certainly was not a whale."[7]

Because Mr. Kermode's views on stranded carcasses will be encountered again, it is appropriate to digress for a moment to examine his rather unusual credentials. Kermode was a controversial figure in the history of the BC Provincial Museum. He started his career at the museum in 1890, at age 16, as an office boy and apprentice taxidermist under the first director, John Fannin; there is then no mention of him in any surviving documents until his appointment as curator in 1904. "There is so little material, in particular so little correspondence, one researcher has concluded that Kermode must have had a bonfire in the late 1930s, leaving in the files only those documents which showed him in a favourable mode."[8] Although one would hesitate to trust Kermode's judgment in matters of delicate zoological identification, he could certainly not be blamed for not recognizing the animal from a partial sample; Carter, a professional zoologist, had seen the whole creature and not recognized it.

The head and some of the flesh, with part of the vertebrae, had been sent to the Pacific Biological Station of the Department of Fisheries in Nanaimo, to be examined by its director, Dr. W.A. Clemens, British Columbia's senior fisheries biologist. From characteristic features of its skin and bones Clemens recognized the carcass as belonging to a basking shark.[9] The basking shark, up to 40 feet in length, is a frequent visitor to B.C. waters, often appearing at the surface, sluggish as a log, and easily approached by boat. The scales on its skin are small and sharp, giving the skin a rough appearance. Its bones are soft and cartilaginous and easily decompose, although its vertebrae are more durable.

This was neither the first nor the last time that decomposing basking sharks were to fool laymen and experts alike. Heuvelmans has presented a number of examples of misidentification of stranded carcasses of basking sharks. Rotting basking sharks lose their softer tissues first and take on a "long-neck plesiosaur" shape (Figures 25 and 26); the fibres of the surface muscles break up into whiskers when the skin rots and the flesh is discoloured.[10]

Over the years, a number of other stranded carcasses have been equally disappointing. For example, a carcass found on Kitsilano Beach, in Vancouver, in 1941, dubbed "Sarah the Sea Hag" by the press, was touted as possible remains of a Caddy. "She had a large horse-like head with flaring nostrils and eye sockets; a tapering, snake-like body 12 feet long; and traces of long coarse hair on the skin." The stinking remains were examined by Dr. W.A. Clemens, who had by then become a professor at the University of British Columbia, and his junior colleague, Dr. Ian McTaggart-Cowan. "We're not sure if it is a basking shark," said Dr. Clemens, "but there is no doubt it is of the shark family."[11]

One who did not agree with this verdict, however, was G.V. Boorman, former first-aid officer at the Naden Harbour whaling station, the scene of the discovery, in 1937, of a mysterious carcass which will be described in detail later. Boorman, then a private in

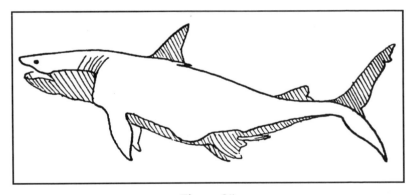

Figure 25.
Transformation of rotting shark into a "plesiosaur" shape. (FROM *HEUVELMANS*, 1968).

Figure 26.
The Skaket Beach (Cape Cod) carcass: a striking example of the process. (FROM HEUVELMANS, 1968).

the army, had examined the stomach contents of 4,000 whales in ten years and was familiar with sharks in various degrees of decomposition or digestion. "If that's a shark, I'll eat my uniform," said Boorman. "I've seen the skeletons of scores of varieties of sharks and they had no resemblance to these remains." He swore that the "marine monster discovered in the stomach of a sperm whale in 1937 was the twin sister of odoriferous Sarah."[12]

In December 1947, Henry Schwarz and three other fishermen found a very large carcass in Vernon Bay, Barkley Sound. They brought much of it back, in sections, to Port Alberni for display and examination. It was described as 45 feet long, with a skull 12 inches across, closely resembling that of a horse or a camel. There were more than 150 vertebrae in the displayed section. Scientists from the Nanaimo Biological Station were puzzled, and talked about it possibly being a ribbon fish. Clifford Carl, a Ph.D. zoologist from the University of Toronto with experience in fishery research, and Kermode's successor at the Provincial Museum, looked at the pictures and immediately guessed that the skeleton belonged to a basking shark.[13] This was also Heuvelmans' opinion when he viewed the published evidence.[14]

Another tantalizing stranding took place on Whidbey Island on September 29, 1963. Mrs. Ruth Cobert reported finding a rotting, 25-foot-long carcass on the shore south of Sunset Beach. The creature was partially buried in the sand and badly decomposed. The 20-inch-long skull resembled that of a horse. The spine was about six inches in diameter at the skull and tapered to two inches at the tail end. Some cartilaginous material accompanied the carcass. Published pictures were interpreted by Dr. A.D. Welander of the University of Washington's Fisheries Department as belonging to a basking shark.[15]

Interest in strandings remains high. Decomposed carcasses are readily declared to be "unidentified monsters", but are usually recognized later for what they are by professional zoologists. A 13-foot-long "marine monster... with a large head and mouth, two fins and tentacles close to its head", found on Gambier Island, Howe Sound, in 1936, was presumably identified quickly since it received no further reference in the press.[16] Another example is that of an animal stranded in 1956 on an Alaskan beach and claimed to be 100 feet long, which was later found to be a Baird whale of more modest dimensions.[17]

There are no remains from any of the above strandings; furthermore, in nearly all cases, there was scientific consensus on the nature of the creature, usually a basking shark. None of the above strandings contribute to the evidence in favour of Caddy's existence. There is one carcass, however, that was not found on the beach, on which there is near-complete agreement that it was not a known animal.

This most intriguing of all carcasses claimed to have been a Caddy was found in the stomach of a sperm whale caught near the Naden Harbour whaling station, Queen Charlotte Islands, in the summer of 1937. Well before people had learned to love them, whales were quite common in British Columbia waters. Humpbacks could regularly be seen frolicking in the Strait of Georgia. Giant baleen and toothed whales, blue and sperm, were commonly spotted offshore. Over much of a century there was a lively whaling industry on the coast. Whalers towed their catches to whaling stations on Vancouver Island and in the Queen Charlotte Islands where they were cut up and rendered for oil. The digestive tracts of sperm whales were also regularly explored for precious ambergris which, at that time, was worth its weight in gold. William Hagelund was a whaler in his youth and has vividly described his summer adventures during the last years of the British Columbia whaling industry in his book *Whalers No More*.

Activity at the Naden Harbour whaling station was concentrated in the summer. Whaling ships (the six "colour" boats, so called because they were all named after a colour) and their crews, as well as the shore teams of flensers, packers and auxiliary personnel, sailed up from Victoria in the spring and stayed until the weather turned stormy in the fall. In 1937, the Consolidated

Whaling Corporation operated two whaling stations in the Queen Charlotte Islands: one at Rose Harbour in the south, the other at Naden Harbour in the north. Three whaling ships were assigned to each. Every day or every few days, depending on the catch, the whaling boats returned to the station to process their prey. The whole operation was under the direction of general superintendent Alphus Dominique Garcin; whenever Mr. Garcin left Naden for Rose, F.S. Huband replaced him as station manager.

In mid-summer of 1937, while opening up a sperm whale caught that same day, the flensers came upon a strange creature in the whale's stomach, a kind they had never seen before and unusual enough for them to alert Mr. Huband, who was in charge at the time. Jim Wakelen was employed at Naden Harbour that summer as a blacksmith. He clearly remembered the event, the excitement caused among the Oriental flensers by the unusual creature and how all station personnel came to gawk at it.

The whale itself had been harpooned and killed by one of the colour boats on the fishing grounds off Langara Island in mid-July. It was towed, via Parry Passage, to the Naden Harbour station and flensed soon afterwards. During the short waiting period (ten to 12 hours, according to Wakelen), some slight digestion of the surface features of the creature may have taken place. However, the body was essentially intact and easily distinguishable from any marine animal previously known to the whaling-station men. It was also totally unlike any other deep-water prey animals, such as the six-gilled shark, ragfish, or giant squid regularly encountered by the flensers when they searched sperm-whale stomachs for ambergris.

Mr. Huband decided the creature was so unusual that some record of it should be made, and he had the specimen prepared for photography. The animal was laid out on a five-foot table on the boardwalk, the top surface lengthened by upended packing boxes; the top of the tables and the elevated background frame were draped with white sheets, suitably positioned behind the head, neck and trunk, to enhance contrast. Prints from the original photographic negatives made by Mr. Huband have been preserved. One of them has already appeared in the press; a copy was also found in the B.C. Provincial Archives.[18] Another, taken from a slightly different angle, was published in Hagelund's *Whalers No More* as a "sea oddity". Captain Hagelund obtained the photo from the Vancouver Maritime Museum, where further research showed it to be part of a folder of 38 photographs attributed to G.V. Boorman, the whaling station's first-aid officer. The last two photos of that folder depict the unidentified carcass as: "The remains of a Sperm Whale's Lunch, a creature of reptilian appearance 10 ft 6 in in length with animal like vertebrae and a tail similar to that of a horse. The head bears resemblance to that of a large dog with features of a horse and the turn down nose of a camel."[19]

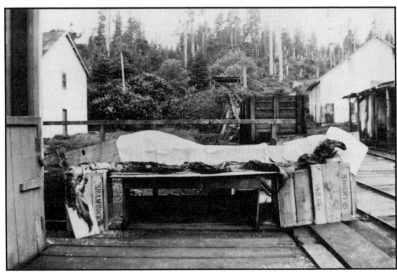

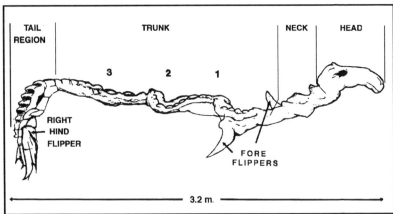

Figure 27.
The Naden Harbour carcass with an interpretation of its features
(G.V. BOORMAN PHOTO).

Figure 28.
Another view of the Naden Harbour carcass. (G.V. BOORMAN PHOTO).

Careful comparison of the Boorman photos with the print attributed to Huband shows that they are different: there are thus three photos of the presumed Caddy carcass, taken with two different cameras. The sharpest pictures are Boorman's: they are shown here as Figures 27 and 28.

The photos allow an estimate of the dimensions of the creature (3.5 to 3.8 m or 11.5 to 12.5 feet) and of its elongated shape and general features. The surface is smooth except in the tail region; there are no large scales, obvious hair-like covering or thick blubber padding visible. The horse-like (or dog-like) head appears to bear traces of an eye and a mouth. The neck appears to have been severely crushed by the killing action of the whale's jaw before it was swallowed whole. There is some evidence of short fore-flippers. No external sex organs are visible. The body is thin (15 cm or 6 inches in diameter) and a mid-dorsal ridge, or crest, is present, consisting of low, rounded tubercles each around six cm or 2.4 inches long at the base; each one of these (there are about 26 in all) may correspond to vertebrae of the spinal column.

The tail is lighter in colour than the trunk and shows a most interesting structure. There appear to be hind flippers located alongside, and apparently fused to the last nine to ten true tail fragments. The indistinct outline of components of the right hind flipper of Caddy corresponds more closely with the position and size of skeletal elements of the same flipper in a Mesozoic plesiosaur than in a modern seal or walrus (Figure 29). The narrow front flippers are probably used as hydrofoils, in surfacing and diving, not for power to propel the animal forward.

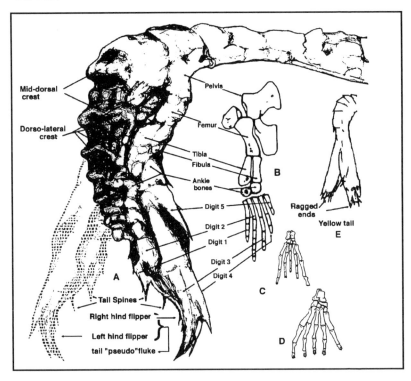

Figure 29.

A. An interpretation of the tail section of the Naden Harbour carcass. The numbers correspond to vertebral segments from the apex of the tail. The presumed left flipper (hidden behind the cardboard in the photo) is shown shaded. The bones of the hind flipper of a plesiosaur (Cryptoclidus) are shown in B, with a possible correspondence to features of Caddy's tail. (FROM NORMAN, 1985). For comparison, right hind flipper skeleta of a seal (Monachus) and a walrus (Odobenus) are shown in C and D. (FROM WYSS, 1989). Also shown, in E, is an interpretation of the tail of Hagelund's baby Caddy shown in Figure 31.

Jim Wakelen was present when the photographs were taken (he remembers Huband, but not Boorman). Another eyewitness description is reported by Hagelund, quoting an old-time whaler, Finn John, who saw the specimen and said that "it had a horselike head with large limpid eyes and a tuft of stiff whiskers on each cheek. Its long slender body was covered by a fur-like material, with the exception of its back, where spiked horny plates over-lapped each other. It had skin-covered flippers and a spade-shaped tail, like a sperm whale."[20]

Quoting from the whaling station's annual report, the *Fisheries News Bulletin* published by the Department of Fisheries in September 1937 referred to the carcass as "about 10 feet long, having a head similar to a large dog's, animal-like vertebrae, and a tail resembling a single blade of gill bone as found in whales' jaws."[21]

In 1937, there was little communication between the Naden Harbour station and the rest of the world during the whaling season. The photographs were probably not developed until much later in the summer since they did not appear in the press until October 31, 1937, when the *Victoria Daily Colonist* featured one of them (Huband's photo, from the same angle as in Figure 28) on its front page, well after the release of the Department of Fisheries report. Nevertheless, word leaked out earlier that something special had been discovered. Exactly how the carcass was disposed of or whether any part of it was preserved is not known. Boorman's photo album contains a note to the effect that part of the carcass was shipped to the Nanaimo Biological Station soon after its discovery, for identification. Nobody there knows anything about it. It may also have been sent to the Provincial Museum, in Victoria. The following item, which appeared in mid-July, was taken by many as the last word on the story:

"MAMMAL NOT 'CADDY'S' SON

"Portions of Sea Monster Sent to Museum Are From Baleen Whale

"A theory advanced in Vancouver that portions of a marine mammal taken from the body of a sperm whale might have been part of a young sea serpent which was an offspring of Victoria's famous Cadborosaurus was definitely exploded today by Francis Kermode, director of the provincial museum.

"Mr Kermode said there was little doubt that the portion of a backbone, the piece of baleen and the portion of skin forwarded to the museum were pieces of a baleen whale, which he believed was of premature birth.

"The pieces were taken from a sperm whale caught at Naden Harbor in the Queen Charlotte Islands.

"The backbone is about six feet long."[22]

Mr. Kermode's unfortunate suggestion in the matter of the Henry Island carcass should be recalled; there is also good evidence, as seen in Figure 30, that people at the Naden Harbour station could recognize a baleen-whale fetus when they saw one. The curator of vertebrate animals at the Provincial Museum at the time was Dr. Ian McTaggart-Cowan, fresh from a Ph.D. in zoology at the University of California. Regrettably, McTaggart-Cowan was absent on field duties on the date of Kermode's press announcement; when he returned to the museum a few days later, no material was available for viewing and nothing had been preserved. When showed the photographic evidence, Dr.

Figure 30.
Fetal baleen whale at Naden Harbour. Holding the carcass are A. Nixon (left) and James Wakelen. James Wakelen Sr., the station accountant, is in front. (COURTESY J. WAKELEN).

McTaggart-Cowan readily admitted that the creature did not look like anything he had ever seen. Enquiries at the museum show no trace of the specimen in materials in hand or in accession records. If the material was ever received, no record was made; it was not preserved, as was usually done for all other specimens: in short, it was not treated seriously at all. Overall, there is a strong possibility that it may have been misidentified. It should be recalled that Kermode's only training in zoology was as a taxidermist, and it is quite possible that he may have mistaken the "tail resembling a single blade of gill bone as found in whales' jaws" mentioned in the Department of Fisheries report, for an actual whale jaw.

These photographs, authenticated by the testimony of a living eyewitness, Jim Wakelen, and by other reports which independently refer to it, are the closest to concrete material evidence that exists for Caddy. The formal description of the species, as *Cadborosaurus willsi*, in conformity with the rules of international zoological nomenclature, is based on these photos.[23]

The capture of what has been described as a very young specimen of Caddy is found in the memoirs of Captain Hagelund. Years after his whaling days, as Hagelund and his family were yachting through the Gulf Islands, they anchored one night in Pirate's Cove, DeCourcy Island. "With my two sons and their grandfather in our centre-cockpit sloop," he wrote, "we spotted a small surface disturbance in the calm anchorage where we had dropped the hook for the night. Lowering the dinghy, my youngest son Gerry and I rowed out to investigate. We found a small eel-like, sea creature swimming along with its head completely out of the water, the undulation of its long, slender body causing portions of its spine to break the surface. My first thought that it was a sea-snake was quickly discarded when, on drawing closer, I noticed the dark limpid eyes, large in proportion to the slender head, which had given it a seal-like appearance when viewed from the front. When it turned away, a long, slightly hooked snout could be discerned."

It was getting dark, but Hagelund and his son managed to capture the animal with a dip net and brought it on board the sloop for examination. "We found that he was approximately sixteen inches long, and just over an inch in diameter. His lower jaw had a set of sharp tiny teeth, and his back was protected by plate-like scales, while his undersides were covered in a soft yellow fuzz. A pair of small, flipper-like feet protruded from his shoulder area, and a spade-shaped tail proved to be two tiny flipper-like fins that overlapped each other."

The small creature was put into a large plastic bucket for the night. Hagelund realized the uniqueness of his catch and resolved to bring the specimen to the Pacific Biological Station in Nanaimo on the following day. "We retired early," he continued, "for I intended to leave at first light, but sleep would not come to me. Instead, I lay awake, acutely aware of the little creature trapped in our bucket. In the stillness of the anchorage, I could hear the splashes made by his tail, and the scratching of his little teeth and flippers as he attempted to grasp the smooth surface of the bucket. Such exertion, I began to realize, could cause him to perish before morning.

"My uneasiness grew until I finally climbed back on deck and shone my flashlight down into the bucket. He stopped swimming immediately, and faced the light as though it were an enemy, his mouth opened slightly, the lips drawn back exposing his teeth, and the tufts of whiskers standing stiffly out from each side of its snout, while his large eyes reflected the glare of my flashlight. I felt a strong compassion for that little face staring up at me, so bravely awaiting its fate.

"Just as strongly came the feeling that, if he was as rare a creature as my limited knowledge led me to believe, then the miracle of his being in Pirate's Cove at all should not be undone by my impulsive capture. He should be allowed to go free, to survive, if possible, and fulfill his purpose. If he were successful, we could possibly see more of his kind, not less. If he perished in my hands, he would only be a forgotten curiosity. I lowered the bucket and watched him swim quickly away in the darkness, then returned to my bunk for a peaceful rest, my mind untroubled by the encounter."[24]

It was only later, when he came across the news clipping of the Naden carcass, that Hagelund realized the similarities between the two creatures. There are indeed many points of similarity between the puny animal of Figure 31, sketched by Hagelund, and the adult Caddy: the long, thin shape, the large eyes, the teeth, the short front flippers. The scaly back is suggestive of the serrations mentioned by Langley and Kemp. Upon later questioning, Captain Hagelund also confirmed his impression that the tail

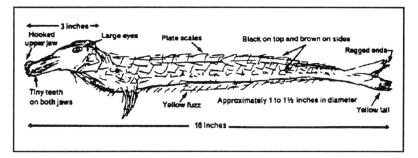

Figure 31.
Hagelund's baby Caddy. (FROM HAGELUND, 1987, COURTESY HARBOUR PUBLISHING).

region of the small animal was formed of two overlapping seal-like flippers, and not a single tail fluke. He also mentioned that he had noticed the flippers separating briefly while the animal was swimming in the bucket on the deck of his boat.

There is another report, somewhat less explicit, of a possible baby Caddy. Retired Seattle pharmacist Phyllis Harsh related how, in the summer of 1991, she had found a live "baby dinosaur" on the beach on Johns Island, near Stuart Island, opposite South Pender Island, on the American side of Haro Strait. She seized the small creature, about two feet long, with sticks and threw it back into the water. She also mentioned having found a "small dinosaur" skeleton beneath a bald eagle's nest, also on Johns Island.[25]

Whether the animal seen by Mrs. Harsh was the same kind as that seen by Captain Hagelund, and whether any one of these was really a baby Caddy, remains a matter of conjecture.

CHAPTER V

JOKES AND HOAXES

Reports of unusual phenomena usually excite fear and incredulity, the latter often expressed by ridicule. It is but a short step from personal ridicule to gentler public humour, and Caddy, like other famous cryptids, soon spawned its own rich crop of jokes, hoaxes, cartoons and fabulous stories. Humour is of course also a powerful way to introduce unusual facts and ideas.

Caddy contributed to this lore from its very first appearance. While the official version of its naming soberly refers to Cadboro Bay and to some possible saurian kinship, there are also reports that Archie Wills later spun, or at least repeated, a story of an Indian legend about "Cadboro, a beautiful Indian maiden who was so lovely that the gods decreed she should remain untouched by man. A reckless Indian brave named Saurus threw caution to the wind and wooed her. The angry god of air and water, in revenge, turned himself into an eagle, carried off Cadboro, punishing her by turning her into a stone, reputedly Gonzalez Hill. Saurus was turned into a sea serpent being sentenced to be banished for a billion years to the depth of the ocean."[1]

Through his long association with Caddy, Wills took pride in "having added something to our reservoir of science and society" and clearly appreciated "his" sea-monster as more than just a zoological mystery.[2] Caddy provided a fertile backdrop for the observation of human behaviour which Wills apparently delighted in.

As one would expect, cartoonists took an immediate and lasting liking to Caddy, often showing it in conversation with its presumed cousins in Loch Ness and Lake Okanagan. Wills was quite defensive about the status of Caddy, insisting in vain that it bore "no relationship to Ogopogo, which is purely a fictitious sea-serpent."[3] Caddy's 1933 sightings near Victoria occurred during a

Figure 32.
Ogopogo rejoices at Caddy's arrival on the scene, with allusion to the provincial electoral campaign underway at the time. Drawing by Jack Boothe. (VICTORIA DAILY TIMES, *21 OCT. 1933*).

Figure 33.
Ogopogo, in the background, jealous of Caddy's notoriety, again with a political sub-theme. (FROM ARCHIE WILLS' SCRAPBOOK).

vigorous election campaign which brought Liberal leader T.D. Pattullo into office. Political cartoonists soon used Caddy and Ogopogo as props. The *Colonist*, having essentially admitted defeat in trying to impose its name (Amy) for the creature, played up the angle of a romance between Amy Cadborosaurus and one Wat Mackintosh, of Loch Ness, to the tune of turgid, pseudo-Scottish verse.

It also took little time for astute advertisers to take advantage of public interest in Caddy. On November 15, 1933, only slightly

Figure 34.
Amy Cadborosaurus meets Wat Mackintosh. (VICTORIA DAILY COLONIST, *7 JAN. 1934*).

more than a month after the Langley and Kemp revelation, the *Victoria Daily Times* announced:

"SEA SERPENT IS CAPTURED"

The subtitle gave the story away: "Well-designed Dummy, 25 Feet Long, Had City Agog This Morning." Victoria furriers L.E. Mallek's and Sons had built a green, wood-and-canvas model of Caddy, complete with tin serrations on its back and a hinged head to induce a bobbing motion in the waves. The creation had been towed out of Victoria's inner harbour before dawn and parked in plain sight near the breakwater. Hundreds flocked to the waterfront to see it. Along with the firm's name, two signs were attached to the structure, carrying the message: "Why Don'tcha Come Up and See Me Sometime."[4]

As early as 1933, the *Daily Colonist* offered a $20 prize for an authentic photograph of Caddy. By 1951, the *Victoria Daily Times* had raised the offer to $200. Although its value gradually increased over the years, the prize was never awarded. By 1981, there was mention of a $5,000 prize "for a confirmed sighting", presumably with a good photograph.[5] A recent enquiry at the offices of the *Times-Colonist*, the successor to both newspapers, confirmed that the offer is no longer current. The first official entry in the *Daily Times* 1951 picture contest was received in mid-April of that year and was submitted by Dr. Clifford Carl, then director of the Provincial Museum. "Here at last is the photo of

Figure 35.
The Mallek model. (VICTORIA DAILY TIMES, *16 Nov. 1933*).

"CADDY" RE-TIRES AT
VICTORIA TIRE LTD.

10-Day MONSTER TIRE SALE

Figure 36.
*Caddy at the service of selling tires. (*VICTORIA DAILY TIMES, *JUNE 1963).*

Caddy which you have been waiting for," wrote Dr. Carl, claiming that he had "surprised the creature in a secluded bay which apparently had been overlooked by other serpent seekers." Upon close questioning, Dr. Carl admitted that the photograph was not genuine, and was a picture of a slightly doctored stick, found floating in the Upper Harbour. "I wanted the money to provide comforts for totem-pole sitters," he jocularly confessed.[6]

Dr. Carl maintained a long-lasting interest in Caddy, examining the evidence and occasionally offering provocative comments. One evening, lecturing to the University Extension Association, he remarked that: "When sea lions frolic off-shore in Victoria waters that is when everyone hears reports of Caddy being sighted."[7]

The Chamber of Commerce reacted explosively. "Caddy is real!" cried its managing secretary, George I. Warren. "Caddy is not a sea lion and Caddy is not a myth."[8]

While he never saw enough evidence to convince him that there was a real Caddy, quipping that "He's to native Victorians what Santa Claus is at Christmas Time," Dr. Carl kept track of Caddy over many years.[9] His scrapbook, kept at the Royal British Columbia Museum, is a valuable record of Caddy's history.

Sober citizens who gather together for holidays and relaxation often indulge in rather juvenile tricks. In May 1963, Vancouver Island druggists, drug salesmen and physicians held a fishing derby at a resort in Mill Bay, Saanich Inlet. One afternoon, there was much activity in a boathouse; hammering and sawing noises were heard. Later in the evening, the derby committee was seen watching and laughing as a contraption of driftwood and tires was towed past the resort's landing floats. Unaware of the fun and games, Miss Nettie Ross, the aunt of resort-owner Tom Brown, innocently snapped two photographs of the sea-serpent cavorting past her cottage window. She described the animal to the press: "It was black, or dark in colour. It looked like an animal and dipped its head many times as it floated along in the bay."[10] It was not long afterwards that, in an incisive display of investigative journalism, a reporter-photographer team, alerted to the possibility of the hoax, discovered the remains of the "monster" in the resort's boathouse. "A cheap publicity stunt," said one of the neighbours. Over the years columnists, especially in Victoria, have adapted Caddy to all occasions. In March 1952, Monte Roberts reported how his wife had interviewed Caddy, then recently seen in Vancouver, and had been reassured that it preferred Victoria waters.[11] One should not be surprised to find, a few days later, a front-page headline announcing:

"CADDY CAPTURED BY PASSERBY IN INNER HARBOR"

The passerby in question, one Kosmos Kagool, a recent immigrant, had lassooed Caddy with a hawser to impress his lady friend. The beast was at that very moment thrashing at the end of that line, available for public as well as scientific scrutiny. The April Fool's joke might have been more compelling if the very "politically incorrect" photo of a chimpanzee had not been used to feature the hero of the story.[12]

It is difficult to ignore the display of faked Nessie photos appearing in the imaginative "news" magazines offered for sale near grocery-store cash registers. The best that one can say about them is that they are indeed very creative in their arrangement and description of "evidence". Caddy has so far not received similar attention, although its potential for mystery and excitement is at least as great as that of its Loch Ness cousin.

"Monte Roberts, please . . . !"

Figure 37.
*Cartoonist Bierman's view of Caddy. (*Victoria Daily Times*, 31 May 1963).*

A journalistic assessment of Caddy's following and of the effect of hoaxes on its reputation is clearly presented by an editorial from the *Victoria Daily Times*:

"CADDY WRITHES AGAIN

"The collapse of the latest Caddy manifestation should not be permitted to dishearten us. For Caddy is much more real than the clumsy attempts made from time to time to give him synthetic bones and flesh of one kind or another.

"Caddy will long outlast his would-be creators, as he will outlast his detractors. He will be sighted innumerable times, but never quite long enough, or quite clearly enough, or quite opportunately enough for a photograph to be taken. No cynical construction of wood or rubber will ever successfully impersonate him, nor will the exposure of such efforts as fraud imperil his reality.

"Even the scientific doubters — the proponents of the floating-log, three-porpoises-in-a-row, kelp-bed, or breaking-wave schools — will fail to weaken the cult of Caddy. For he relies for his permanence not on eye-witnesses or photographs, not even on the reasoned logic or scientific lore of the experts. Indeed, Caddy's most devoted believers are those who have never ever caught a glimpse of him and probably never will. There is a Caddy because there ought to be one — and that is proof enough for anyone."[13]

Thus, in spite of the good humour it always generated, Caddy could not just be laughed away as a joke. People continued to see it and were convinced that they had not seen any textbook marine animal. Humour and publicity helping, many people have come forward with unreported stories. The press continued to provide the public forum for cryptozoological reports and discussion.

CHAPTER VI

WHAT IS CADDY?

So, what is Caddy? Is it really a mysterious creature, glimpsed but yet undiscovered, a magnet for the curiosity of natural scientists, or is it merely some by-product of human error and imagination, a topic more worthy of the attention of psychologists? A wide range of explanations has been offered.

When reporting Caddy sightings, people may be lying; they may be making errors of interpretation; or they may be providing an accurate description and interpretation of what they have seen. Lies include hoaxes, a more imaginative and whimsical form of the genre. Errors may include mistaking inanimate objects for live ones, as well as not recognizing known animals. Through pre-selection of testimonial evidence, lies, hoaxes and errors should have been eliminated from the data base (Appendix I). Nevertheless, so many skeptics insist that all evidence falls into these categories that they must be discussed too.

Liars normally expect some benefit from their actions: undeserved rewards, an escape from punishment, fame and respect. Most Caddy witnesses admit to being suprised, even somewhat embarrassed by what they saw; they are usually reluctant to talk about their experiences, and have often been subjected to the ridicule of their family and friends. This is not much incentive to or benefit from lying. Witnesses have shared their confusion and bewilderment; none of those who confided their experiences struck the researchers as potential liars. Thus, lying is an unlikely explanation for Caddy sightings.

Hoaxes are lies of a different ilk, usually with humorous rather than malicious intent, although sometimes also perpetrated with some benefit in mind. Broad public interest in Caddy almost immediately prompted practical jokes and clever advertising. Most hoaxes are quickly uncovered, and sooner or later revealed, although some, like the Piltdown Man, may have long-lasting effects. Although there have been a few Caddy hoaxes, the sightings are too numerous, and too many seem genuine, to dismiss Caddy as merely a hoax played by a few clever jokers.

Then, of course, there are possible mistakes and misinterpretations. Every elongated animal, singly or serially, has been put forward at some time as an explanation for Caddy. Caddy sightings have been attributed to conger eels, humpback whales, elephant seals, ribbon (or oar) fish, basking sharks and sea lions. Unfortunately, none of these animals closely resemble what is reported as Caddy. One frequent and sometimes plausible explanation for a Caddy sighting, advocated by Clifford Carl and others, has been the sea-lion family, with the large bull in the lead, followed by his harem. For example, two provincial police officers, Inspector Robert Owens and Staff Sergeant Jack Russell, saw a "huge sea serpent with a horse-like head" in the Strait of Georgia, off Qualicum Beach. "With a pair of binoculars Sgt. Russell saw that the strange apparition was a huge bull sea lion leading a herd of six sea lions....Their undulations as they swam appeared to form a continuous body, with parts showing at intervals as they surfaced and dived. To the naked eye, the sight perfectly impersonated a sea monster."[1] A particularly embarrassing case, where a pair of mating sea lions was mistaken for Caddy, involved Chuck Ball, Art Stewart and three others, who had set out in a boat to investigate a Caddy seen by more than 25 observers on the beach north of Qualicum Beach. The bull sea lion aggressively snorted at them, unhappy to be disturbed in its amorous frolics.[2] Sightings where a group of sea lions might be involved have been eliminated from the data, and in most cases, the features and the behaviour of Caddy are clearly not those of a sea-lion family.

Although it is difficult to generalize on the basis of a few isolated sightings, the screened reports collectively provide a large and essentially consistent data base from which an idea of Caddy's physical appearance, distribution and behaviour can be gained. Whatever Caddy may be, then, it should conform to what the data say about it. To sum up the evidence, Caddy's most striking features are:

1. Its dimensions, ranging from five to 15 metres in length;
2. Its body form: snake-like, or serpentine, with extraordinary flexibility in the vertical plane;
3. The appearance of its head, variously described as resembling that of a sheep, horse, giraffe or camel;
4. The length of its neck, elongated, ranging from one to four metres;
5. The vertical humps or loops of the body, arranged in tandem series directly behind the neck;
6. The presence of a pair of anterior flippers; posterior flippers absent or nearly fused with the body;
7. The tail, dorsally toothed or spiky, and split horizontally or fluke-like at the top;
8. The very high swimming speed, clocked at up to 40 knots at the surface.

In addition, there are numerous details which provide additional clues about Caddy's nature, but are not always present or mentioned. Sometimes the back is described as serrated, sometimes as smooth. This feature was deemed quite relevant in early Caddy observations; Penda, observed by Cyril Andrews and his friends at Pender Island, was thought to be different, perhaps in gender, from the Victoria-area Caddy because it did not have a serrated back. Body colour is reported as ranging from "gunmetal" blue, through orange, green, brown, gray to black. Fur, fuzz, or hair on the neck or body is sometimes mentioned, "like that of a seal", or "like coconut fibre"; most often, however, the skin is described as smooth. Some witnesses see bumps on the head, which they variously describe as ears or horns, sometimes both together. Most mention eyes, sometimes large, sometimes coloured. There is also occasional mention of facial whiskers.

No known creature, living or fossil, conforms to the description of Cadborosaurus in more than a few, and never in all eight, of the major features which distinguish it. A visual comparison of Caddy with major marine contenders (Figure 38) illustrates how strikingly different it is in body form. Others have already attempted

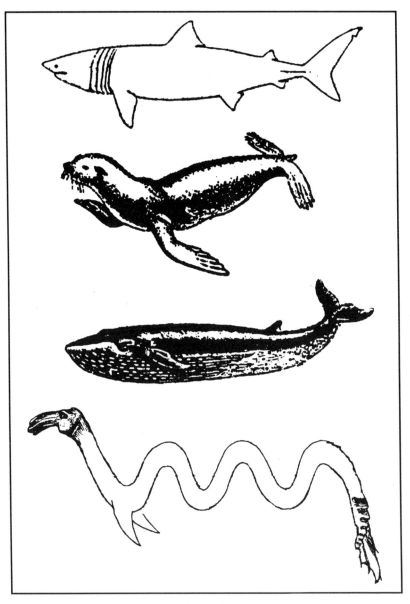

Figure 38.
*Caddy compared to other marine animals: basking shark; sea lion; baleen whale;
Cadborosaurus. (Not to scale).*

Figure 39.
Heuvelmans' merhorse. (FROM HEUVELMANS, 1968).

Figure 40.
Heuvelmans' long-necked sea monster. (FROM HEUVELMANS, 1968).

to group all Caddy features into a synthetic creature. Figure 12 was an early attempt, perhaps more artistic than zoologically inspired. Heuvelmans, in his voluminous review of world-wide sea-serpents, grouped together all the "elongated sea-animals of large size characterized by a medium length neck, a mane, a horse's head and large eyes" under the label "Merhorse", and offered a sketch (Figure 39) in which some of Caddy's features, especially its head and neck, can be recognized.[3] A closely related variant is Heuvelmans' "Long-necked" sea-monster, distinguished from the merhorse mainly by the length of its neck (Figure 40). There is thus some consensus on the appearance of Caddy and on how it differs from other large marine creatures.

Habitat

Each sighting in the data base has been assigned to one of six areas: 1 Juan de Fuca Strait; 2 the southern Gulf Islands; 3 Saanich Inlet; 4 the Strait of Georgia; 5 other near-shore areas; and 6 offshore — outer coast or open ocean areas. The numbers of sightings in each area and season are presented in Table I.

TABLE I

Distribution of sightings by area and season

Area	1	2	3	4	5	6	All
Winter (JFM)	16	8	6	13	3	1	47
Spring (AMJ)	15	8	2	10	5	2	42
Summer (JAS)	8	5	8	9	6	5	41
Fall (OND)	14	8	1	2	5	5	35
Undated	4	0	0	9	2	2	17
Area Totals	57	29	17	43	21	15	182

Caddy is seen most frequently inshore (Areas 1-5), particularly in eastern Juan de Fuca Strait and the Strait of Georgia. The density of observers along the coastline is far from uniform, and these statistics may thus be biased on that account. This possibility must be kept in mind when interpreting the data.

Table I does not show any clear seasonal preference in Caddy's appearances, but perhaps it is more sensitive to climatic than to calendar seasons. B.C. waters essentially experience two "seasons".[4] The winter period begins with the "fall transition", some time in October; the Aleutian low-pressure system dominates the atmospheric circulation and spawns a series of storms which buffet the coast with strong southeasterly winds, accompanied by cloudy skies and heavy rainfall. Occasional outbreaks of cold polar air over the Coast Range break the monotony, bringing snowfall followed by periods of frigid blue skies. Winds and cold air keep surface waters cold (less than 10°C) in all near-shore areas. Around April, the Aleutian Low weakens, winds shift to northwesterly, and long periods of sunny weather and lighter winds lead to warming up of surface waters (in some places, reaching 20°C) in the summer period. In some areas, where tides are particularly strong, such as in eastern Juan de Fuca Strait and in the narrow passages between Vancouver Island and the mainland, surface waters are continuously mixed with colder, deeper layers and never become very warm, even during the summer. Of the selected areas, 1, 2 and 6 (Juan de Fuca Strait, the Gulf Islands and offshore) show the least seasonal variation in water temperature, while the other areas, particularly 3 and 4 (Saanich Inlet and Strait of Georgia) are covered by a significantly warmer surface layer (three to ten metres deep) during the summer season.

The distribution of Caddy sightings between the cold (October to April) and the warm (May to September) seasons (Table II) shows that there are clearly more sightings in the former (101 to 64). However, while Caddy obviously prefers cold areas (Areas 1,2,6) and is most often seen during the cold season, it does venture into warmer areas (Areas 3,4,5), where it is seen with about equal frequency in the cold and warm seasons.

TABLE II

Modified seasonal distribution

Area	1	2	3	4	5	6	All
COLD (O-A)	36	21	8	19	11	6	101
WARM (M-S)	17	8	9	15	8	7	64
Undated	4	0	0	9	2	2	17
TOTAL	57	29	17	43	21	15	182

At this point, it may be noted that sperm whales hunt well below the sea surface, in depths reaching 1,000 metres and more, where water even colder (2 to 5°C) than that observed at the coast is found all year. That would have been the habitat of the Naden Harbour juvenile. In view of this fact, and of the distribution of sightings, Caddy is assumed to be a cold-water creature, living most of its life in water masses ranging from 5 to 12°C, found in well-mixed coastal waters (for example, Juan de Fuca Strait), upwelling areas (in the summer, on the west coast of Vancouver Island) and deeper offshore layers (200 to 2,000 m). Nevertheless, Caddy also ventures into warm areas during the summer and has even been seen on the shore.

Swimming

Caddy is a strong swimmer and moves very quickly, both above and below the water surface. When swimming at the surface, the body often forms into one to five or more vertical humps or loops in tandem directly behind the neck. These loops have been reported to move at exactly the same speed, each at a constant height above the surface, with a constant distance between them. The musculature ripples in a continuous motion "like a travelling wave moving from head to tail",[5] traversing all loops. No side-to-side, snake-like undulations have been observed. The small, paired, pectoral flippers are rarely seen above the surface; they may serve as hydrofoils for controlling body elevation at high speed, or for sudden submergence, as required. The tail flippers appear strongly webbed and nearly fused with the tail in a shape which would resemble, but be more flexible than, the tail fluke of a whale, and would be similarly effective as a propulsive paddle. The digitation and webbing of the tail flippers is similar to that of frogs, which provide thrust using both feet simultaneously rather than alternately.

The swimming mechanism is not yet well understood. One might think that, because of its snake-like shape, Caddy would propel itself in an undulating motion, as do eels and sea snakes, although in the vertical rather than horizontal plane. The principal thrusting action would almost certainly be generated by the powerful fluke-tipped tail or hind flippers. Frictional drag on Caddy's long body would restrict this form of motion to rather slow speeds, however forceful the driving actions of the tail region might be. [6]

Other fast swimmers, like tuna, or orcas, have a powerful caudal paddle, with a relatively short, streamlined body. How can Caddy, with such a long body, reach the high swimming speeds ascribed to it? One way to reduce frictional drag is to decrease the effective length of the body by bunching it together in loops, transforming it into a shape more closely resembling that of a tuna and other fast-swimming fish (Figure 41). In that configuration, the loops

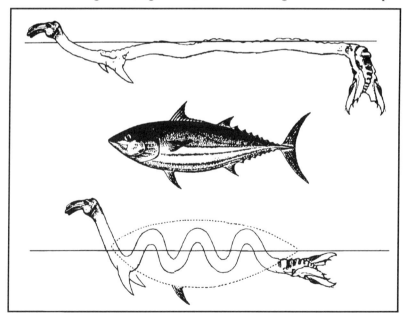

Figure 41.
Stretched out (at the top), Caddy would be an inefficient swimmer. Bunched up in loops, its body would approximate that of a tuna (middle), a very fast swimmer.

would be in each other's wake and the total friction between the body and the water would be much reduced. When Caddy is swimming at the surface, this shape transformation would also place a good part of the body in the air, with a further reduction of friction, allowing the powerful, fluke-like tail to drive the shortened body at great speed by an up-and-down motion. This kind of locomotory body transformation remains untested and would be unique in large animals; while it would require a special locking mechanism of the vertebral column to maintain its form, it would also provide Caddy with a definite advantage in feeding and in escaping predators.

Feeding

The presence of strong jaws and sharp teeth suggests a carnivorous lifestyle. A number of reports mention Caddy feeding on salmon or in herring beds; there have also been numerous instances of bird-snatching. The relatively small size of the head and the long, slender neck would presumably restrict the size of its prey to small and medium-sized fish, squid and perhaps shrimp, in addition to sea birds. On the other hand, the reported breadth of its head and jaws suggests that it might be capable of larger prey. Its high swimming speed would enable it to capture fast-swimming species, like salmon, mackerel, small tuna and squid, while avoiding potential predators like orcas and sperm whales and possibly the great white shark and giant squid. Caddy's large eyes and whiskers presumably function in detecting and capturing deep-swimming fish and squid, in the "twilight zone" of mid-ocean depths.

Respiration

Although Caddy is only rarely seen at the surface, all indications are that it is an air-breather. Several observers have described nostrils at the snout end of the head, and some have described "steam" or "jet" emissions from them. Others have mentioned noises: hissing, blowing, whooshing and even mooing sounds. Because the trunk region is slender, except in very large individuals, the lungs would have to be elongated, as in snakes and lizards. However, the fact that Caddy is so rarely seen indicates that it does not come to the surface very often, and that it might be capable of holding its breath for a very long time, as some marine mammals can.[7]

The possibility that Caddy might possess some secondary aquatic respiration mechanism, allowing it to replenish its oxygen supply under water, and perhaps remain submerged indefinitely, has also been proposed.[8] What appears as a mane might actually not be hair, but some gill-like, gas-exchange organ. These long, hair-like filaments have been described as reddish in colour, suggesting a possible haemoglobin content. Another possibility is that Caddy might, as has been suggested for sea snakes, be able to extract oxygen directly from the water through the body wall.[9] In that case, its elongated shape would be an advantage, a large surface-area to volume ratio for optimal gas exchange.

Hot or Cold-Blooded?

Caddy is long and narrow in shape and does not appear to be bolstered by thick layers of insulating blubber, as whales are. Given the high surface-area to body-volume ratio associated with this shape, it would be difficult for Caddy to maintain the high body temperature typical of mammals (35 to 38°C) in its cold-water habitat. Internally regulated temperature balance (homeothermy) under such conditions would necessitate near-constant feeding and enormous conversion of food energy to compensate for the rapid loss of body heat. In cold-blooded animals (poikilotherms) on the other hand, like fish and reptiles, body temperature is not kept at a constant high level by an internal thermostat and may adjust to that of the surroundings. If Caddy were such an animal, it would require little energy for heat production and thus need a relatively lower rate of food intake. High energy production might then be conserved for use in short bursts, such as rapid pursuit of prey, or eluding potential predators. Metabolic rates could also remain relatively low, on average, with lesser demands on respiration and hence rarer appearances at the sea surface. Recent research on fish has shown that temperature regulation may be limited to essential parts of the body, such as the brain.[10] Deep-diving mammals also have special adaptations in their circulatory system: blood is shunted from less crucial organs to lessen heat loss and maintain the flow of oxygen to the brain.[11] It is not unreasonable to think that Caddy's lifestyle might be accompanied by similar adaptations to its environment.

Reproduction

If Caddy is well adapted to its cold environment, it might avoid the warmest coastal areas, except in special circumstances. Its appearance in warm surface waters during summer, and its rare presence on land, could be associated with a particular kind of need. Reproduction comes to mind — an extremely important aspect of life in all living beings, and one often accompanied by unusual behaviour. All that is known about reproduction in Caddy is that:

1. There are smaller individuals seen with larger ones: possibly their offspring, but also perhaps their mates;
2. A small individual was found within a whale's stomach;
3. A very small individual, probably a baby, was caught (by W. Hagelund) and another one, perhaps, was seen at the shore (by P. Harsh); both in relatively warm water. If these very small individuals are correctly associated with the larger ones, their size and where they were found might provide more clues about Caddy's nature.

The baby-Caddy specimens observed by Hagelund and Harsh were very small compared to the adult creature, and not found in the vicinity of an adult, suggesting that Caddy is born ready to function and receives little attention from its parents. Young animals which are fully developed and independently active at birth are called precocial; in contrast, those which are incompletely developed and helpless, such as the young of many birds and mammals, are called atricial. Reptilian precocial young seldom receive post-natal care from the mother, except in crocodiles, a few snakes, and perhaps in some advanced dinosaurs. Reptilian precocial young (for example, baby turtles) are typically tiny in relation to the size of the mother, whereas precocial young of mammals (for example, colts, fawns, whale calves) are relatively large. In perspective, the human species lies somewhere between these categories, but is essentially atricial.

Do baby Caddies come from eggs or are they born alive? Mammals do not lay eggs; sea-snakes and other cold-blooded aquatic reptiles (except turtles and crocodiles, which lay eggs in naturally heated nests) also bear their young alive: they are viviparous. This is also probably the case for Caddy. It does not have hind flippers suitable for digging a nest on the shore in which to lay eggs. The cold waters in which it lives are not suitable for incubating eggs. Most aquatic reptiles, as well as most other higher aquatic vertebrates, such as mammals, go ashore or into shallow water for reproductive purposes on an annual or seasonal basis. Seals do so in large rookeries; grey whales congregate in warm lagoons. No such breeding concentration of Caddies has ever been seen. Going ashore singly, at night, in quiet areas, might be what Caddy does, and might account for sightings on shore, or in warm areas during the summer, as well as for the presence of babies seen in warm waters near the shore. This is of course quite speculative.

What Kind of Animal?

What conclusions can be drawn from these observations and inferences? The data are far too sparse and soft to use the more mathematical techniques of biological classification. One convenient method of placing Caddy in relation to other kinds of large marine animals is by comparing primitive and advanced characteristics of observed properties.[12] There are eight traits, listed in Table III, for which evidence, or inference, can be brought to this

TABLE III. CLASSIFICATORY FEATURES OF AQUATIC VERTEBRATE ANIMALS: COMPARISON OF CHARACTER STATES

TAXON	Body Size SM. LGE.	Body Shape REG. SERP	Head & Neck SML. LGE. LNG SHORT	No. legs 4 2 0	Tail Style VERT. HORIZ.	Thermal Physiol. CB. WB.	Reproduction Location PR.AQU. TERR. 2ND AQU	Type OV. OVOV. PLAC.	P/A INDEX
A. *Cadborosaurus*	2	2	0	0+	2	0?	2?	1?	9?
B. Bony Fishes	0+	1	2	0	0	0	0	0+	3+
C. Amphibians	0+	0+	2-	1	0	0	1	0+	4+
D. Mod. Reptiles	0	2	0	1	0	0	1	1	5
E. Plesiosaurs	2	2	0+	0+	0+	1?	2?	1	8+?
F. Primitive Mammals	0	0	2	0	2	2	1	0+	7
G. Pinnipeds, Advanced Mammals	1	1	1+	1-	2-	2	1	2	11
H. Cetacea	2	0	2	1	2	2	2	2	13

LEGEND: 0 = plesiomorphic; 1 = intermediate; 2 = apomorphic; +, - some members with other character states
? - probable but uncertain

process. For each one of the characteristics listed in Table III, a number from 0 to 2 is attributed to a group of animals (or taxon) according to whether it has primitive (0) or advanced (2) qualities. For example, in the category "body size", small is primitive and receives a zero score, while very large is advanced and receives a two. Caddy receives a two in that category, as do dinosaurs and cetaceans. Under "thermal physiology", cold-bloodedness rates a zero, while warm-bloodedness receives a two. The other categories are described in the legend of the table.

Overall, Caddy ranks most closely with marine saurischian (plesiosaurs) or thalattosuchian (marine crocodilians) reptiles and marine mammals, which is perhaps not too surprising. To be more definite, one has to weigh the relative importance of the various characteristics.

Some researchers, like Heuvelmans, have emphasized the more mammalian aspects of this kind of creature, in particular the presence of hair, and sometimes of a mane, and the vertical flexure of the spine in swimming motion. The form of the hind flippers, particularly as seen in the Naden carcass, is also suggestive of a mammalian, perhaps a pinniped relation. What looks like hair may, as noted, be something else. On the point of vertical flexure, although no living reptiles are capable of bending their spines in a vertical plane, the similarity between the vertebrae of modern whales and of Jurassic marine crocodilians *Steneosaurus* and *Metriorynchus* (Figure 42) shows that the latter were also capable of vertical flexure, so that this feature might not by itself be sufficient to characterize an unknown animal as a mammal.[13] Caddy's vertical flexibility is indeed extraordinary among large vertebrates. The webbing of the hind flippers is also found in some aquatic reptiles, crocodilians, for example.

The thinness and elongation of the body, the poikilothermy (or cold-bloodedness) which it seems to imply, and the great difference in size between the young and the adult are strong points in favour of a reptilian nature.

In the light of the available evidence and of some reasonable inferences, the tentative classification is that Caddy is a reptilian animal, although with some mammalian traits. We have formally described it, on the basis of the Naden Harbour photograph, as *Cadborosaurus willsi* (in honour of Archie Wills), a "new species representative of an unnamed subcategory of reptilia", perhaps

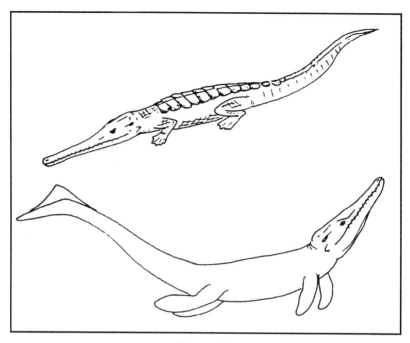

Figure 42.
Early marine crocodilians. (BUFFETAUT, 1983).

most closely related to the extinct marine reptiles shown in Figure 42. Such a classification, based on partial information, is always subject to revision when additional evidence becomes available. Nevertheless, a formal description is often necessary to set the stage and initiate informed discussion and research on the subject.

Finally, it is important to note that it is not impossible that more than one unknown animal might be hiding under the label "Caddy". That idea arose as early as when Cyril Andrews and his friends reported an animal without the serrated back typical of earlier Caddy descriptions. At that time, a differentiation in terms of gender was proposed. Perhaps it was thought then that one kind of sea-monster was all that public credulity would stand. Heuvelmans nevertheless suggested two kinds of animals to explain global observations of animals of this kind: the merhorse and a "long-necked" sea-serpent, much like a seal but with a very long neck, seen in Figure 40. The current data are not sufficiently detailed to justify creating two different cryptid species.

CHAPTER VII

CADDY'S COUSINS

Large, serpentine, aquatic animals have been reported from other parts of the ocean and from lakes. Heuvelmans, in his world-wide survey of sea-serpents, puts Caddy together with similar merhorses observed mainly in the North Atlantic, off the coast of North America as well as in waters around northern Europe.

A solid and detailed sighting from eastern Canadian waters is that of the "sea-giraffe", seen in 1913 from the bridge of the steamer *Corinthian* as it was crossing the Grand Banks of Newfoundland. The second officer, G. Batchelor, and the quarter-master, Mr. Ayres, observed the animal at length. In Batchelor's words:

> "Suddenly... something surprising showed itself about two hundred feet away from the ship.
> "First appeared a great head, long fin-like ears and great blue eyes. The eyes were mild and liquid, with no indication of ferocity.
> "Following sad eyes came a neck, it was a regular neck all right, all of twenty feet in length which greatly resembled a giraffe.
> "The monster took its time in emerging, but it kept emerging so long that I wondered what the end would be.

"The neck...seemed to be set on a ball-bearing, so supple was it and so easily and rhythmically did it sway while the large liquid blue eyes took in the ship with a surprised, injured and fearful stare.... Three horned fins surmounted its bony head.... The body was about the same length as the neck very much like that of a monster seal or sea-lion with short water-smoothed fur.

"The tail was split into two small fins."[1]

Mr. Batchelor's description and sketch of the creature (Figure 43) are reminiscent of Caddy reports, although there are also many significant differences.

The habitat of Caddy-like creatures may thus not be limited to the west coast of North America, and probably also not to coastal areas, although that is where they are most often seen. While it is not surprising to find that a large, fast-swimming, marine animal should have a very broad distribution, it is surprising to find reports of a similar creature in lakes, sometimes quite far from the sea. Yet, Caddy-like creatures have been reported from a great number of northern-hemisphere lakes, the best known being Loch Ness in Scotland, Lake Okanagan in western Canada, Lake Storsjön in Sweden, and Lake Champlain in eastern North America, where live, respectively, Nessie, Ogopogo, the Storsjöodjuret and Champ. This is not the place to present a critique of the quality of the information on the cryptids seen in those lakes. While photographic evidence has been produced in favour of the famous creatures listed above, it is sometimes controversial.[2] Comparable reports from eyewitnesses do, however, suggest some resemblance between Caddy and its potential fresh-water cousins.

Loch Ness is one of the lakes which occupies the Great Glen of Scotland, a major feature cutting through the Scottish Highlands. The lake is about 30 kilometres long by one kilometre across and about 300 metres at its deepest. It connects with the sea through the short River Ness at its eastern end. It has been claimed that the creature's history goes all the way back to 580 A.D., when St. Columba was preaching to the Picts, and there have been many recent sightings as well as intense scrutiny of the loch and of its presumed dweller.[3]

On the basis of 250 eyewitness observations, the Loch Ness "Monster" is described by Mackal as being 20 to 25 feet long, with

Figure 43.
The sea-giraffe seen by Mr. G. Batchelor, second officer of the CORINTHIAN, on the Grand Banks of Newfoundland, 30 Aug. 1913. (FROM DAILY SKETCH, LONDON, 25 SEPT. 1913).

observed humps on its back ranging from one to three; there is some evidence for forward flippers; horns and a mane are reported in about five percent of the sightings. Most observations make no references to eyes. The descriptions of Nessie are rather vague and lacking in detail compared to those of Caddy. There are some reports of animals with a head like that of a sheep, or a snake, but many are simply of "dome-like" objects rising above the water.

Ogopogo inhabits Lake Okanagan, a nearly 100-kilometre-long body of water with an average width of about two kilometres and a maximum depth of about 250 metres. Witnesses speak of a creature with a head variously resembling that of a cow, a horse, a snake, or an alligator, with a long (sometimes up to 75 feet) serpentine body. There have been reports of a pair of protrusions on top of the head. Ogopogo is also reputed to be a very fast swimmer. Indian legends mention the animal and describe it as amphibious.[4]

The Great Lake (Storsjön is Sweden's fifth-largest lake) lies 292 metres above sea level. It has an area of 456 square kilometres. The animal, Storsjöodjuret, has been mentioned since the Middle Ages and there are rune stones that are supposed to depict it. Seen from a distance, the Great Lake Monster of Sweden resembles a long, serpent-like creature with humps and a small, dog-like head, with fins or ears pressed against the neck. Its length varies from 3.5 to 14 metres and its width from one to 1.25 metres. The few witnesses who have seen the creature at close range describe it as short and chubby, about three metres long with short thick feet, a large head and round eyes. The animals makes wailing, whining and rattling sounds. Its skin is variously described as smooth, slimy, and sometimes scaly. It swims very quickly.[5]

Champ lives in Lake Champlain, the largest of these four lakes: 170 kilometres long, up to 15 kilometres wide in places, with a maximum depth of 120 metres. The lake is between Vermont and New York states; it reaches into Canada at its northern end. Champ is dark in colour, serpentine, about 20 feet long, and is described as having one to three humps, with a snake-like or horse-like head.[6]

There is undoubtedly some general similarity between the descriptions of all these creatures and of Caddy. If these reports reflect a similarity in fact and possibly some kinship, one must wonder at the presence of these animals in these lakes (and possibly others). Most northern areas of the Earth were covered by a giant ice sheet about 10,000 years ago. There certainly were no Caddy-like creatures in those lakes at that time: the lakes themselves were not there; only a multi-kilometre thick ice sheet. The ocean, however, remained hospitable. Caddy creatures could have migrated into the lakes in the past few thousand years, after the melting of the ice. That would certainly have been very easy to do from the North Sea to Loch Ness: a few kilometres without waterfalls or rapids. It would be much more difficult to reach lakes far inland, such as Okanagan or Storsjön. Perhaps the much larger rivers which existed during the most active period of glacial melting would have made that trek easier. Caddy has been sighted in fresh water (the Fraser River, Harrison Lake), and one might imagine its hungry ancestors chasing salmon up rivers and finding themselves trapped. If that is so, and this is of course just a hypothesis, information about lake cryptids becomes pertinent to knowledge about Caddy. Reports about Caddy, many of which have been summarized here, are much more detailed in terms of anatomical information and realistic animal behaviour than those from lakes; the study of lake cryptids might thus profit from data about their possible oceanic relatives.

CHAPTER VIII

WHAT NEXT?

"When sometime a true sea serpent, complete and unde-
cayed, is found or caught, a shout of triumph will go through
the world. 'There you see', men will say, 'I knew they were
there all the time. I just had the feeling that they were there.'
Men really need sea-monsters in their personal oceans. ...An
ocean without its unnamed monsters would be like a
completely dreamless sleep."

John Steinbeck
The Log From the Sea of Cortez

How can anyone be absolutely sure that Caddy is there? If
absolute certainty means being able to touch the animal and study
it at will, it is necessary to capture a specimen. It would certainly
be much easier, although perhaps less spectacular, to capture a
baby Caddy, as Captain Hagelund did, than an adult. Before
being able to consider seriously a baby-Caddy-finding expedition,
it may be necessary to find out more about Caddy's nature and
habits. After all, fishermen have been casting their nets for years
in the waters where Captain Hagelund's specimen was caught.
Considering the costs of operating at sea, it might be wise to
improve the odds over blind chance by learning more about the
subject. There are also important moral issues about capturing

wild animals which may make it desirable to study Caddy at a distance, without ever capturing it.

There are some, perhaps, who would insist that Caddy should continue to be enjoyed as a mystery: that once known and classified it would become just another animal in a zoology textbook; that we all need mysterious sea-monsters in our "personal oceans". Holders of this point of view need not worry for some time: full revelation will not happen tomorrow, and mystery will long continue to surround Caddy. Curiosity, however, cannot be thwarted and will relentlessly foster investigation. Knowledge does not eliminate awe; scientists, who explore nature's secrets, also usually feel deep wonder at its beauty and complexity and devote their entire lives to its worship. People should thus look forward to a day when Caddy becomes as well known, and as well loved, as whales are today.

There are two parallel paths to learning more about Caddy and eventually to lifting it from the realm of cryptozoology, the study of hidden, doubtful animals, to that of zoology proper. The first consists of continuing to record, systematically, every appearance of Caddy, so as to gradually enhance the body of knowledge about its characteristics, behaviour and distribution. For this to happen, there has to exist a sufficiently receptive atmosphere of public and scientific interest, so that witnesses will feel comfortable revealing their experiences. Caddy-watch exercises and organizations for collecting Caddy reports can play a significant role in creating a suitably friendly climate.

The second path involves experimentation. Science advances by exploration and by experiment. Exploration includes passively waiting for things to happen as well as searching for what's new; it leads to discovery by chance. Experiment, on the other hand, leads to discovery by design. An experiment is a procedure for testing a hypothesis. One has an idea about how the world works and tests it. For example:

Hypothesis: the Moon is made out of green cheese;

Test: go to the Moon and find out.

More subtle hypothesis: Einstein's general relativity theory claims that heavy objects, such as the Sun, deflect light rays which pass very near them;

Test: during an eclipse of the Sun, observe the apparent position of stars very near the Sun's disk and look for a small change from ordinary conditions.

All information about Caddy has so far come by chance: exploration by opportunity. It is necessary to consider how knowledge could also be gained by experiment, by testing hypotheses about what Caddy is and what it does. Of course, it is not always obvious just how to formulate a testable hypothesis, and one may have to fumble for some time before learning anything, particularly in circumstances where one has no control over what happens.

An experiment consists of stating precisely what one expects to see (the hypothesis), and carefully designing observations to find out whether this happens or not (the test), even when one can't control all the experimental conditions. One outcome of the experiment may be that the hypothesis is confirmed: things do happen as one thought. The tendency would be to rejoice: we were right! For example, Archie Wills suggested that Caddy was attracted to Victoria waters by the abundance of salmon. If this is used as a hypothesis, the data indeed reveal that there are many Caddy observations in early fall, at the time of some large salmon runs. That is not much to rejoice about, however: if Caddy sightings occur at other times of the year, what explains its presence then? Couldn't Caddy show up during salmon runs for the same reasons it shows up at other times of the year and not necessarily for the salmon? A positive result doesn't teach us much: only that the hypothesis is compatible with observations, along with perhaps dozens of others.

Given the status of knowledge about Caddy, confirming a hypothesis about its nature and behaviour may still be a useful result, which may guide further exploration and testing. For example, from the capture of presumed baby-Caddy specimens in warm water during summer months, and from the sighting of a Caddy onshore, it is inferred that Caddy, while preferring cold waters, may venture into warmer, inshore, perhaps intertidal, areas to give birth to live babies, which it immediately abandons to this presumably benign environment. Such behaviour might be associated with the tidal range, which controls access to the shore. Darkness may also be preferred. The hypothesis based on this idea provided a focus for a Caddy-watch initiated during new-moon, summer spring-tides in 1993. That Caddy was not spotted at that time, however, neither confirms nor denies the hypothesis, since it is easily argued that Caddy could have come and gone unnoticed.

One learns most by stating a hypothesis in the negative. For example: "Caddy is never seen except at some specific times: those of some salmon runs." Any one observation at any other time immediately falsifies the hypothesis. That simple statement can then be dismissed as an explanation of Caddy's presence.

The trick is to formulate a hypothesis which truly reveals something new. That indeed is the scientific challenge of Caddy, a challenge that is daunting far beyond the material rewards which it offers, but nevertheless is a puzzle of natural history worthy of the attention of the cleverest minds.

This book has summarized what is known about Caddy today. Dear reader, it is now up to you.

LIST OF CADDY SIGHTINGS

This is our data base of eyewitness reports; it includes only sightings which satisfy two criteria: the object seen must be unambiguously alive and clearly not a known animal, because of its appearance or dimensions. While we have searched extensively through the British Columbia press, and widely broadcast our interest in this subject over many years, we cannot claim that this list is comprehensive. Indeed, we know of additional reports which we have not included here, either because we could not be convinced that they satisfied our criteria, or because we could not trace back their source.

Sightings are presented in chronological order in the following format:

date (year, month, day, or season, as available), place (area code)
names of witnesses
features observed
source of information

Area codes are attributed as follows: 1- Juan de Fuca Strait: from Chatham and Discovery Islands westwards; includes all Victoria and Cadboro Bay sightings; 2- Gulf Islands: Canadian and US Gulf

Islands north and east of Juan de Fuca Strait; 3- Saanich Inlet; 4-
Strait of Georgia: east of Gulf Islands to Cape Mudge; 5- Other
inshore waters; 6- Offshore: outer coast, Queen Charlotte Islands.

Statistics on seasonal and spatial distribution are presented in
Tables I and II in the text. The distribution of sightings by decade
is shown in Figure 13 of the text.

Oft-quoted sources are abbreviated and followed by a date: e.g.
TIM 5 Oct. 1933 (*Victoria Daily Times*, etc.). Similarly, other newspapers: *Victoria Daily Colonist* (COL), Victoria *Times-Colonist* (VTC),
Vancouver *Sun* (SUN) and *Province* (PROV), the *Sidney Review* (SID),
the *New York Herald Tribune* (NYHT). Earlier surveys: Heuvelmans,
1968 (HEUV), LeBlond and Sibert, 1973 (L&S), Archie Wills' scrapbook (WILLS). Letters or calls to the authors, ELB and PHL.

1881 Summer. Nanaimo (4)
Frank Stannard "folds"
PROV, 24 Aug. 1940.

1884 Oct. 27. Tacoma (5)
John M. Barker
"sea pet", 60 ft long, four ft thick; horns on its back
Seattle *Post Intelligencer*, 10 Aug. 1951.

1895 Spring. Between Seattle and Juneau (6)
L.H. Titus from steamer *Willapa*
"reptile" head 10 ft above water, 18" across;
much faster than boat; body 24" across.
PROV, 21 Jul.1943.

1895 Oct. 26. Bellingham Bay (5)
Seventeen people
Immense dark body, 150 ft long
20-30 ft. neck
Seattle *Times Magazine*, 26 Oct. 1975.

1897 Jun. 26. Queen Charlotte Islands (6)
Osmond Fergusson
long neck, 25 ft long body
D.Mattison, *B.C.Historical News*, 17, #2, 1964.

1905 Summer. Johnstone Strait (5)
Philip Welch and one friend
Long neck; knobs on head
L&S

1909 Oct. 2. Off Santa Barbara, CA (6)
Steamship *St. Croix*
60 feet long, head like eel, thick as a man
San Francisco *Examiner*, 2 Oct. 1909.

1910 Apr.10. Saanich Inlet (3)
Two fishermen
Quick look, hideous monster
TIM, 11 Apr. 1910.

1912 August. Johnstone Strait (5)
Mrs.Hildegarde Forbes
snake-like, 40 ft long, mane like seaweed; 5-7 humps
HEUV p. 445.

1917 July. Near Jordan River (1)
R.M. Elliott
8 ft neck, like giraffe, 4-5 humps; shot at it.
TIM, 19 Oct. 1933.

1919 August. Mill Bay, Saanich Inlet (3)
Mary Lebel
Large green hump
Letter to PHL, 19 Dec. 1988.

1922 May 22. Malcolm Island (5)
C.G. Cook
long neck, large eyes, 25 ft long
L&S

1923 Victoria (1)
W.B. Grant
huge head, two eyes in front, whiskers,
brown and shaggy
WILLS

1925 Cape Mudge, Strait of Georgia (4)
J. Nord and Peter Anderson
head like camel, 2.5 ft across, whiskers & mane
fangs 6-8 in. long in mouth; fin on its back
TIM, 17 Oct. 1933.

1926 Oct. Tahsis Canal (5)
native fisherman
Huge creature with long neck
COL, 16 Apr. 1967.

1926 Aug. West of Queen Charlotte Islands (6)
Capt. Obman, Fred Ellisas, B. Oban
15 ft body out of water, immense head
Columbian, New Westminster, 26 Aug. 1926.

1927 Sep. Fulford Harbour, Saltspring Is. (2)
Arthur E. Johnson & several others
seasonal appearance; after schools of fish
TIM, 14 Oct. 1933.

1928 late fall. West of Vancouver Is. (6)
James F. Murray
head like a horse and lengthy neck
TIM, 4 Jan. 1954.

1928 Aug. 24. Chatham Sound (5)
A.J. Sprague (Fish Commissioner)
300 ft long, greenish blue, 4 ft across
shot and hit it
Empire, Juneau, 19 Feb. 1992.

1928 Harrison Lake B.C. (4)
two men
40-50 ft long; 8 in diameter
Belle Rendall; "History of Harrison Lake..." 1981
Harrison Lake Historical Society, Canyon Press, Hope, BC.

1930's (early). Willows Beach, Victoria (1)
Betty Fraser
undulating form, head higher than body
Letter to ELB, 12 Aug. 1993.

1932 10 Aug. Chatham Is. (1)
F. Kemp
large, serpentine, serrated back
TIM, 5 Oct. 1933.

1932 Roberts Creek (Sunshine Coast) (4)
Hubert Evans, Dick Reeve, Bob Stephens
horse's head, eye bumps, nostrils, ears/horns
long neck, 12 inches through
H.White, *Raincoast Chronicles Six/Ten*, p 276-278
Harbour Publishing, 1994.

1933 early June. Gabriola Is (4)
W. McAllister
spouted water from mouth.
TIM, 19 Oct. 1933.

1933 Aug. 6. Burrard Inlet (4)
Mrs. Edith M. Clark
head like big seal and three humps;
three times length of rowboat
TIM, 20 Oct. 1933.

1933 Sep. 23. Cadboro Bay (1)
Mrs Dorothea Hooper & neighbour
"like gable of house floating in water"
TIM, 24 Oct. 1933.

1933 Oct. 1. Chatham Island (1)
W.H. Langley and family
80 ft long, serrated back, camel-faced
TIM, 5 Oct. 1933.

1933 Oct. 12. Trial Island. (1)
Mr & Mrs R.H. Bryden
dirty green; serrated back like a fan;
spouting water with gushing sound
TIM, 23 Oct. 1933.

1933 Oct. 14. Chemainus (2)
Don Bellamy, George Neil, Harry Olson
lying on top of water; left wake like speedboat
TIM, PROV, 17 Oct. 1933.

1933 Oct. 14. Oak Bay (1)
C.F. Eagles
head, neck, coil, tail total 60 ft
crocodile-like, spines on back
COL, 15 Oct. 1933.

1933 Oct. 21. Race Rocks (1)
Capt. W.N. Prengel, First Off. J. Richardson.
SS *Santa Lucia*
"upturned barge" but moving rapidly; wake of foam
TIM, 21 Oct. 1933.

1933 Dec. 3. South Pender Island (2)
Cyril Andrews, N. Georgeson, K. Georgeson and 8 others
swallowed duck in front of Andrews
head like horse, no ears or nostrils
head three feet long and two feet wide.
TIM, COL, SUN, 6 Dec. 1933.

1933 Dec. 4. Chatham Is. (1)
Ellwood White
head like horse, three humps, 40 ft long
SUN, 7 Dec. 1933.

1933 Dec. 21. Plumper Sound (2)
Cyril Andrews, Arthur Pender
color of ling cod; no serrated back
TIM, 9 Jan. 1934.

1934 Jan. 5. Fraser River, foot of Main St.,Vancouver (4)
Murray Jackson, Billy Alexander, three friends
four foot neck, cow-like head, two horns or ears
SUN, 8 Jan. 1934.

1934 Jan.7. Trial Is. (1)
C.and E. Marsh and J.W.Chilton
gobbled seagull, camel-like head
TIM, 9 Jan. 1934.

1934 Jan. 18. Bedwell Harbour, Pender Is. (2)
Cyril Andrews, Arthur Pender, Eileen McKay;
40 ft long; feeding on herring; gulls picking at it;
dark stripe along back; not serrated; face flesh
coloured; no whiskers
TIM, 23 Jan. 1934.

1934 Mar. 29. Victoria, off the breakwater (1)
I. McGavin; H. Sagar
Two animals (Caddy and Penda)
TIM,1 Apr. 1934
NYHT, 23 Apr. 1934.

1934 May. Seymour Inlet, Nakwakto Rapids (5)
Sam Dumaresq, Tom Lynch, Ed Lynch
long neck at 40° angle
Letter to PHL, 22 Nov. 1987.

1934 May 26. Off Cape Flattery (1)
Capt. Landstrom, First Officer Connolly,
SS *Dorothy Alexander*
head as large as 40-gallon barrel
TIM, 27 May 1934.

1934 Sep. 11. Patricia Bay, Saanich Inlet (3)
May Williams
giant snake-like monster battling with black ducks
head like giant snake, 4-5 feet out of water, 4-5 coils
SID, 12 Sep. 1934.

1936 Apr. 11. Cadboro Bay (1)
Arthur P. Dawe, Mrs Dawe, Joe Smith
camel's head, three distinct "undulations"
dived; came to surface to blow;
PROV, 17 Apr. 1936.

1936 Apr. 12. Lummi Is. (5)
Tugboat crew; Ole Kavande, Eddie Cadger
35-40 ft long; two ft through; dark grey
swimming at 10 knots
PROV, 18 Apr. 1936.

1936 Saturna Island (4)
E.J. Stephenson, wife, son
three feet thick, yellow and bluish
sliding over the reef
Advance, Langley, B.C., 22 Apr. 1960.

1937 Jan. Devil's Churn, Oregon Coast (6)
William and Ila Hunt
long neck, giraffe head, mane
L&S

1937 Campbell River (4)
Mr. W.W. Taylor
five coils, 35 ft long, 1.0-2.5 ft across
very fast swimmer.
Letter to ELB, 23 Aug. 1993.

1937 Cadboro Bay (1)
Mrs M.K. Cole
brownish, horse-like head, long neck
Letter to PHL, 14 Jan. 1985.

1937 Feb. 5. Clover Pt., Victoria (1)
Mrs Fraser Biscoe
heading towards Oak Bay; no good description
TIM, 6 Feb. 1937.

1937 Apr. 30. East of Gabriola Is. (4)
crew of barge *Etta Mac*
body 18" thick; mouth full of teeth;
stripe brown and yellow; friendly eye
TIM, 30 Apr. 1937.

1937 May 2. Off Jordan River (1)
Mr & Mrs G. Meynell, Miss D. Meynell, Mrs C. Belcher
huge serpent: "glorified green garter snake"
TIM, 4 May 1937.

1937 early Oct. Queen Charlotte Is. (6)
Fisheries Department notice
10 ft long with horse-like head
Prince Rupert *Daily News,* 18 Oct. 1937.

1938 Aug. 11. West Vancouver (4)
Dorothy Burniston and George Wragg
20-50 ft long; noisy; humps (by moonlight)
SUN, 12 Aug. 1938.

1938 Nov. 13. Oak Bay (1)
"two local residents"
long head, jaws, fin on back
COL, 16 Nov. 1938.

1938 Dec. 6. Chemainus Bay (2)
Crew of *Catala Chief* (coastal tug)
William Y. Higgs, George R.Macfarlane and John Shaw
One large, (40ft) one slightly smaller; vertical
oscillations; snake-like head; round body
PROV, 8 Dec. 1938.

1939 Off Columbia River (6)
Chris Anderson, Jacob Lind
camel head, 10 ft neck
John Grissim, *National Fisherman*, June 1991.

1939 Mar. 10. Victoria (1)
Mr. Jamieson
20-30 yards long; 35 knots; 5 bumps
PROV, 10 Mar. 1939.

1939 early Mar. Chemainus (2)
Billy Shillito
puffing/snorting; 30 ft long, five humps,
head like horse; spray like speedboat
SUN, 17 Mar. 1939.

1939 late March. Satellite Channel (2)
Bob Gaetz, Frank Marshall & Bill Smith
One large (40 ft); head bigger but like horse's
one smaller one too; hair on head & body
chestnut brown; no fins
PROV, 31 Mar. 1939.

1939 Apr. 25. D'Arcy Is. (2)
Reginald Parris, Edgar Green
colour of kelp; head like horse; useless photos
TIM, 28 Apr. 1938.

1939 May 14. Nanaimo harbour (4)
Robert Morton, Thomas Hodgson, William Devlin
light brown, horse-like head, large eyes
hissing sound; 20 ft long; 18"across
PROV, 15 May 1939.

1939 May 14. West Vancouver (4)
Jeannette Gannonx and mother
three humps, as long as Dundarave pier
SUN, 15 May 1939.

1939 Summer. Cadboro Bay/Telegraph Bay (1)
Mrs C.E. Tildesley
Long neck
L&S

1939 July. Oregon Coast, 90 miles SW Columbia Riv. (6)
Einar Lovvold, Harold Christensen
Neck & upper part 25 ft out of water
No mane, all grey.
Letter to PHL, 26 Jan.1988.

1939 July. Off Destruction Island, Washington coast (6)
P. Sowerby, R. Menzies, J. Layfield
Big head and eyes.
L&S

1940 Jan. 7. Victoria (1)
Cecil Burgess, Norm Ingram
light brown; whiskers; long neck
SUN, 8 Jan. 1940.

1940 early July. Pat Bay, Saanich Inlet (3)
C.O. Biscaro & W.F. Hinde
yellow head; fins all over the body
PROV, 12 Jul. 1940
COL, 14 Jul. 1940 (photo of witnesses).

1940 mid Oct. Trial Is. (1)
Walter Pratley
bulky head and hump
PROV, 15 Oct.1940.

1940 mid Nov. Pender Is. (2)
Roy Duesenbury
head like horse, two blunt horns
40 ft long, short neck, sound like rush of wind
PROV, 19 Nov. 1940.

1941 Jun. 23. Strait of Georgia (near Brechin) (4)
T. Liston
20 ft long, 6-8 ft across, 2 ft fin on back
like a seal but much longer neck
PROV, 3 Jul. 1941.

1942 Long Beach Washington (5)
Frank E. Lawton
Picture. 16 ft long; large flippers, brown hair
Letter to PHL, 19 Nov. 1987.

1943 early Jan. Mill Bay, Saanich Inlet (3)
Mr & Mrs W. Gibson
long thin neck, humped back; lunged at gulls
PROV, 14 Jan. 1943.

1943 Apr. 15. Granthams Landing (Howe Sound) (4)
S. Spencer & wife plus friend Mrs. Fisher.
head like python; 5-6 coils; 30-40 ft long,
1.5 ft across at thickest
PROV, 21 Jul. 1943

1943 late August. Roberts Bay (near Sidney) (2)
Jan S. Easson.
8 ft long; line of moving spines, 4" high;
undulating up and down
Letter to PHL, 10 Dec. 1969.

1944 Feb. 8 . Keats Is, Howe Sound (4)
William F. Read
large head, two humps
PROV, 11 Feb. 1944.

1944 Feb. 20. Witty's Lagoon, Victoria (1)
Eliz. Rhodo & husb.
40-100 ft long; 3-4 coils; ate sea birds
Call to ELB, Oct. 1992.

1944 Apr. 2. Bazan Bay (near Sidney) (2)
Mrs.A.W. Collins & Mrs. Burt-Martin
four humps, dark coloured
PROV, 4 Apr. 1944.

1944 Jul. Hornby Is., Str. of Georgia (4)
W.Laurence Garvie
Head like sea-horse, nostrils, eyes, ears
snorting sounds, 35 ft long
Letter to PHL, 12 Dec. 1987.

mid-40's Burrard Inlet (Indian Arm) (4)
R.E. Homewood & wife
Whinny-like sound; thick neck; horse's head
no eyes or mane seen
Letter to PHL, 29 Mar. 1988.

mid-40's. Cape Lazo, Str. Georgia (4)
Harold Hayes Jr., Alex Somerville.
head like camel with two knobs like horns
Comox District Free Press, 17 Mar. 1949.

1945 Early Feb. False Creek, Vancouver (4)
W.J. Beattie & J.W. Wakeford
airedale head; grabbed at duck; 10 ft long
PROV, 3 Feb. 1945.

1945 Dec.19. Cordova Bay, Victoria (1)
Tom Plimley, wife, + 2 others
camel coloured; long neck, broad hump; quite long.
PROV, 20 Dec. 1945.

1946 Jan. Powell River, Str. of Georgia (4)
Dona Morgan and Mrs. McAndrew
Horse head
Letter to PHL, 25 Jan. 1988.

1946 24 Jun. Str. Georgia, Comox (4)
Mrs. S.H. Grist
Long neck, horse's head, red eyes; watching her dog.
Letter to PHL, 9 Dec. 1969.

1946 July. Stuart Channel (2)
Ron Winkelman and parents
horse-head, mane, ears, large round eyes
Letter to PHL, 9 Nov. 1989.

1946 Fall. North end of Saltspring Island (2)
Mrs. Dorothy Nilsen
head like sheep; one loop seen;
moved fast after school of fish
L&S

1946 Hecate Strait (6)
Capt. House, Fishery Patrol
like 30 ft telephone pole
HEUV p.473.

1947 Feb. Siwash Rock, English Bay (4)
Peter and Helen Pantages, Chris Altman
Horse face, big eyes, 2-3 humps
Letter to PHL, 30 Jun. 1971.

1947 late Apr. Lyall Harbour, Saturna Island (2)
Mr. & Mrs. Fred Jackson
head like camel or giraffe
SID, 20 Apr. 1947.

1947 May 16. Spanish Banks (4)
Frank McPhelan and Ron Kinloch
blunt head; pointed formation above eyes resembling
horn; Big coil
Seattle *Post Intelligencer*, 20 May 1947.

1947 late Sep. Mill Bay, Saanich Inlet (3)
Mr. & Mrs. George O. McKay
Immense forehead, mouse coloured, no eyes or ears
15 ft long
TIM, 22 Sep. 1947.

1947 Sep. 26. Off Sechelt (4)
Marjory Tupper and Wilma Young
head like horse but no ears, hump
PROV, 29 Sep. 1947.

1947 Nov. Off Ucluelet, Vancouver Is. (6)
George W. Saggers
four-ft neck; jet-black eyes, dark brown mane,
wart-like rather than hairy
COL, 23 May 1965.

1948 Spring. Saxe Pt. Park, Victoria (1)
H.R. Johnston
"Plesiosaur": small head, long neck, very large body;
dark green; emerged, visible two minutes,
Letter to ELB,18 Aug. 1993.

1948 late Jun. Puget Sound, Useless Bay (5)
Rodney R. Hegelson
50 ft long back, serrated. Picture
Letter to PHL, 8 Aug. 1992.

1949 Apr. 12. Ucluelet Arm (5)
Fisherman
large, heavy snouted head, brownish yellow
COL, 13 Apr. 1949.

1949 Apr. 15. Cordova Bay, Victoria (1)
L. Tillapaugh, J. Corner
like large eel, 25 ft long
noise like steam jet, bright orange brown
SUN, 18 Apr. 1949.

1950 Departure Bay, Nanaimo (4)
Mrs. R.H. Leighton
Horse's head minus ears
L&S

1950 Feb. 7. Deep Cove, Saanich Inlet (3)
Mr.& Mrs. K. Stuart Wakefield
moving log like giant snake
TIM, 9 Feb. 1950.

1950 Feb. 5. Victoria (1)
Judge James T. Brown, wife, daughter
looked like monstrous snake
TIM, 8 Feb. 1950; *Macleans*, 15 Jun.1950.

1950 mid Feb. Oak Bay (1)
Fred Maycock and Edward Heppell
"strange-looking creature"
TIM, 22 Feb. 1950.

1950 late Feb. Sidney (2)
Joe Mason
no details
SID, 1 Mar. 1950.

1950 near Mar. 8. Tofino (5)
Gwen Coleman and Bryan Tickle
50 ft, fins 4 ft high, cat-like head, long slender neck;
COL, 8 Mar. 1950.

1950 near Apr. 19. Sidney (2)
Mrs Dan Butler, Mrs H. Bradley
small head like a giraffe
brown, 40-50 ft long
SID, 19 Apr. 1950.

1950 Nov. 17. Victoria (1)
Naval officer
snake-like head,18" across, large teeth,
large flippers, flat tail, not serrated back
large black eyes 2.5-3" across
TIM, 21 Nov. 1950.

1950 Dec. 1. Victoria (1)
Mr & Mrs A.B. Didsbury
8 ft neck,12" across, brown, sort of mane
COL, 2 Dec. 1950.

1950 Dec. 24. Oak Bay (1)
Doreen & Colin Andrews
flat head, 4-5 ft of neck;
Call to ELB, late 1992.

1951 Jan. Victoria area (1)
"seen by 20 people over past month"
COL, 16 Jan. 1951.

1951 Friday before Mar. 31. Victoria (1)
Miss B. Morley, Mrs.D.W. Painton
big square head, three shiny black humps
TIM, 31 Mar. 1951.

1951 Jul. 21. Brentwood Bay, Saanich Inlet (3)
J. McIntyre
brown with dirty brown hair covering long neck
like camel with large eyes
COL, 22 Jul. 1951.

1952 Feb. Esperanza Inlet (Tahsis) (5)
Fish Camp manager & family
eel-like neck, 16-ft long; whale size body,
flippers and flukes; mouth & teeth
COL, 16 Apr. 1967.

1952 Mar. 20. English Bay (4)
Reg Palmer, Bruce Mitchell
20-ft long, big eyes, horse's head three ft long
SUN, 26 Mar. 1952.

1952 Apr 14. Victoria (1)
Fraser Stanford
body appeared smooth from one side, but with
spikes when turned in other direction
TIM, 17 Apr. 1952.

1953 Feb. 12. Qualicum Beach (4)
R.D. Cockburn,C.P. Crawford and R. Loach + two others
dog-shaped head with two "horns"; neck like giraffe
TIM, 14 Feb. 1953.

1954 Jan. McKenzie Bight, Saanich Inlet (3)
Ian M. Sherwin and Herbert Winship
Horse-like head; forward-looking, bulgy eyes
Up-and-down motion; no fins visible
Letter to ELB, 24 Aug. 1993.

1954 Nov. 20. Victoria (1)
Jack Dailey & Jack Salsbury
head like frog: bulgy on top; fawn-color
TIM, 11 Jan. 1955.

1955 Jan. 2. Sooke (1)
Thomas and Marion Smith
head like boxer dog, horns or horse-like ears
jet-black and shiny; body 18" across & serpentine
TIM, 3 Jan. 1955; COL, 4 Jan. 1955.

1955 Jan. 10. Victoria (1)
Mr. and Mrs. S.M. Hobbs; J.M. Wyper
light brown, nose about foot long
TIM, 11 Jan. 1955.

1956 Victoria (1)
E.F. Spence
40-ft long, long neck, eyes
L&S

1956 Monday before Feb. 8. Deep Cove, Saanich Inlet (3)
Mr & Mrs C.F. Dalton and 5 others
dived when planes overhead
SID, 8 Feb. 1956.

1956 Sep. 25. Oak Bay, Victoria (1)
G. Kemperlink, and S. von de Witz-Krebs
Thirty feet long; "revolving fins".
TIM, 25 Sep. 1956.

1957 Jul. 7. Str. Georgia (4)
N. Erickson
horse-like head
L&S

1957 Aug. Zeballos Arm (5)
Un-named man
12 ft long neck
COL,16 Apr. 1967.

1957 Sep. 13. Indian Arm, Burrard Inlet (4)
Job and Cecilia Smith
Indian name Sayn-Uskih = Awful Snake; no details
SUN, 18 Sep. 1957.

1958 late Apr. Whidbey Island (2)
John Oosterhoof + several others
12 ft long, one foot thick
HEUV p 507.

1958 late Sep. Victoria (1)
M. McCord
Small horse's head; 3 humps; beard, barking
L&S

1958 (or 59) July. Brentwood Bay, Saanich Inlet (3)
Mike Johnson
single vertical loop like tire, 2" thick
split tail tip
Call to ELB, Aug. 1993.

1959 Jul. 19. Race Rocks (1)
Cameron family
jagged dorsal crest, fast swimmer
SUN, 24 Jul. 1959.

1959 late Nov. Discovery Is. (1)
David J. Miller and Alfred Webb
long neck; hair like coconut fiber, big eyes
L&S

1960 Mar. 29. Smith Bay near Crofton (2)
Everett Wilson and Scotty Henderson
25-ft long, 4-5 humps; large black eyes
Cowichan *Leader*, 31 Mar. 1960.

1960's many occasions. Alberni Inlet, near Tzartus Island (5)
John Monrufet, crew and passengers of *Lady Rose*
20-ft long, makes great turmoil in water
COL, 2 Feb. 1961.

1961 mid-March. Dungeness Spit (1)
M. Stout, sister-in-law and children
long neck, mane
L&S

1961 Feb. 8. James Island (2)
John Walker
20-ft long, dark brown, hump on back
SID, 8 Feb. 1961.

1961 near Mar. 29. Off Sidney (2)
Mrs. A.R. Stacey
Head moving; seagull eaten?
SID, 29 Mar. 1961.

1960's West Vancouver (4)
W. Kennedy
serpentine head, foot across, grey-brown, smooth-
haired, like seal
Letter to PHL, 9 Mar. 1988.

1962 Dec. 15. Lantzville (4)
W.G. Clarke and Mrs. Clarke
round, ball-like head; film
TIM, 18 Dec. 1962.

1962 Dec. 26. Lantzville (4)
Mrs. R. Guy and Mrs. K.B. Holland
head like camel; big lips; large hump
TIM, 30 Dec. 1962.

1963 Feb. 12. Stuart Channel (2)
Mr. & Mrs. David Welham
picture; like giant eel; uniform grey colour
TIM, 15 Feb. 1963.

1963 near Mar.7. Shelter Pt., Campbell River (4)
Mrs. Tom Conrod
25-ft long, dark grey, coils
TIM, 7 Mar. 1963.

1963 Apr. 18 . Victoria (1)
Mrs. Andy Gilstein
20 ft long, humps, colour of porpoise
TIM, 15 Feb. 1963.

1963 Apr 17. Victoria (1)
un-named couple
dark greenish; like eel; snorting heavily
TIM, 18 Apr. 1963

1963 Mar. 2. Off Gabriola Is. (4)
Mr. and Mrs. R.A. Stewart
huge head, gaping maw like hippo, no teeth or ears
WILLS

1968 Feb. 13. J de Fuca Str. (1)
J. Scott
Blew from mouth- steam. Long neck
L&S

1969 Oct. 8. Cadboro Bay (1)
Mrs W.S. Foster and neighbours
5 ft long, dark green, round lizard-like head
dubbed "Fidele": Caddy juvenile
TIM, 8 Oct. 1969.

1969 Fall. Ucluelet (5)
Wesley R. McCurdy
32-ft long, dark brown, head like seal
long fin on back, spines 8" apart, Sketch
Letter to Biology Dept, Univ. Victoria, 18 Feb. 1990.

1971 Summer. Westport WA (5)
Rea E. Avery Jr.
6-8 ft neck, eyes, mouth; gray; curious
Letter to PHL, Nov. 1971.

1972 Sunday before Apr. 7. Victoria (1)
Carl Hergt, Patricia Macdonald,
brownish, eyes like alligator, lots of bumps
WILLS

1977 Sep. 10. Bainbridge Island, Puget Sd (5)
Ruth E. Kutz & family
log that raised up; grey neck;
Letter to PHL, 7 Feb. 1983.

1978 August. West Coast Vancouver Island (6)
Fred Pearson
turtle-like with long neck; Sketch
Letter to PHL, 26 Feb. 1988.

1979 Feb. Harrison Lake, B.C. (4)
R.E. Probert
"dragon chasing goose"; telephoto shot
Letter to ELB, Aug. 1992.

1979 Oct. Whidbey Island, WA (2)
Kathryn Schaff & husband
blowing every 5 minutes; looking like a huge
diver wearing a helmet.
Letter to PHL, 26 Jul. 1988.

1981 late spring. Yellow Pt. (2)
Gordon Thompson & wife; Saanich
30-ft long, 2 low humps, head & neck
Call to ELB, 24 Jul. 1993.

1981 late June. Sooke (1)
Rudy and Wally Ewert
greyish brown, no fins, fast swimmer
VTC, 29 Jun. 1981.

1982 Aug. Secret Cove, Sechelt (4)
Louise Sanders
like submarine periscope; 6-ft neck;
small ears; colour of wet seal
call to PHL, 23 Oct. 1992.

1983, early spring. Pender Harbour (4)
G. Goff.
seen from airplane, large mass moving slowly
took up whole width of entrance to Gunboat Bay
Call to PHL, 15 Dec. 1987.

1983 Nov 2. 20 miles north of San Francisco (5)
Marlene Martin, Steve Grant, Steve Bjork
100-ft long big black hose 5 ft in diameter
humps moving vertically in wave like motion
John Grissim, *National Fisherman*, June 1991.

1984 Jan. Spanish Banks (4)
J.N.Thompson
20 ft long; tan colored head; giraffe like stubs;
large floppy ears; eyes; mouth; sketch
Letter to PHL, 22 Jul. 1985.

1985 Jan. 3. Str. of Georgia, Gibsons (4)
C.Q. Cole
turtle-like with long neck; sketch
Letter to PHL, 14 Jan. 1985.

1985 late Dec. Sidney (2)
Al Molberg, Sidney
head and neck visible
Call to ELB, 1992.

1986 June. Chatham Is (1)
Geoffrey Hewett
20-ft long, humps.
Letter to PHL, 11 Mar. 1991.

1986 Jul. Off Seward, Alaska (6)
Eric Anderson
Head six or seven feet above water;
serpentine body trailing behind
Letter to ELB, 21 Apr. 1994.

1987 Mar. 1. Becher Bay (1)
Capt. G.Stephen Bain
3 coils; sonar image!
Letter to Museum and call to ELB, 1991.

1987 Mar. 28. Roberts Bay (1)
Richard Smith and Ken Kilner
60-ft long, 2 large blue-gray coils.
Letter to ELB, 1 Aug. 1992

1987 Jun. 1. Active Pass (2)
O.J.& Ruby Garner
15-20 ft. dorsal fin, bulgy eyes, sketch
Letter to PHL, 14 Mar. 1988.

1990 Jul.-Aug. Cook Bay, Texada Is (4)
Frank Corbet, Whonnock, B.C.
20 ft long; large head 2 ft above water
Call to ELB, 1 Aug. 1992.

1990 Summer. Johns Is. Passage, San Juan Is. (2)
Phyllis Harsh
large head, 4-5 ft above water, 2 coils
Call to ELB, Aug. 1992.

1991 Mar. 30. Roberts Creek (Sechelt) (4)
Sheila Bromley & relatives; Richmond, B.C.
50-ft long, head, neck, 2 coils, large animal
Call to ELB, 5 Aug. 1992.

1991 Late Jun. Ardmore Pt., Saanich Inlet (3)
Terry Osland
30 ft animal on beach; slithered quickly to sea
scrape mark and foul odour
VTC, 31 Jul. 1993.

1992 Jan. Gray's Harbor, WA (5)
Doris Sinclair
5-6' neck; swim-dive motion
letter to PHL, 20 Jun. 1992
Pacific Northwest, Seattle Apr. 1993.

1992 May. 15. Cadboro Bay (1)
Prof. John Celona and daughter Marjie, Victoria
head, neck; two low coils.
VTC, 20 Aug. 1992
Letter, to ELB Aug. 1992.

1992 Jun. 14. Cadboro Bay (1)
Michael Timney, Victoria
Several vertical coils, 20-23 ft.
Call to ELB, 1992.

1993 early Feb. Brentwood Bay, Saanich Inlet (3)
Bevan Langton, Victoria
Head small, horse-shaped, 3-4 ft out of water
moving fast, leaving wake.
Call to ELB, Aug. 1993.

1993 May. Maple Bay (2)
Mrs. Patrick Cooney, Duncan,B.C.
15-20 ft long, 2 humps
Call to ELB, 1993.

1993 Jul. 14. Brentwood Bay, Saanich Inlet (3)
James Wells and Don Berends
Two Caddys, 30+ft long, 2 low coils, gun metal
blue; swimming faster than 40 mph
VTC, 28 Jul. 1993.

1993 Jul. 26. Squally Reach, Saanich Inlet (3)
Harold Aun, wife & two friends, Victoria
viewed with 20X scope 30-ft animal
splashing action, submerged after 15 min
Call to ELB, 3 Aug. 1993.

1994 Mar. 19. Str. Georgia, off Fraser R. (4)
Capt. Thomas Ackman
large Caddy-like creature, 40 yds away
head and part of neck for a few seconds
Call to ELB, Apr. 1994.

1994 May 5. Ten-Mile Pt. Victoria (1)
Ryan Green and Damien Grant
blackish head, two truck-tire size humps
VTC, 6 May 1994

1994 May 5. Cadboro Bay (1)
Ron Minchin & wife, Victoria
two low blackish humps
Call to ELB, May 1994.

1994 Jun. 7. Clover Pt. Victoria (1)
Mrs. Ruth Rodgers and husband, Victoria
head and 6 ft long hump
Call to ELB, 1994.

Readers are invited to contribute additional information or criticism on
the above sightings or on events which may have escaped our scrutiny.

APPENDIX II

STRANDINGS/CAPTURES

1930 Nov. 10. Glacier Is., near Valdez
skeleton entombed in ice
24-ft long, tail 14 ft; head 55" x 36"; seven ribs on
each side; 2 flippers, five fingers.
some flesh preserved in Cordova "for scientists".
perhaps whale, but not certain
Daily Alaska Empire, 28 Nov. 1930.

1934 Nov. Henry Island (near Prince Rupert)
badly decomposed remains on beach
skin like sand paper; 30-ft long
backbone; examined by Dr. Neal Carter
(identified as basking shark)
TIM, 22 Nov. 1934
PROV, 23 Nov. 1934
SUN, 26 Nov.1934
London *Illustrated News*, 15 Dec. 1934.

1937 Jul. Naden Harbour
10-ft long "juvenile" found in sperm-whale stomach
Fisheries Bulletin, Ottawa,Sept 1937
PROV, 23 Jul. 1937 (Kermode's quote)
PROV, 16 Oct. 1937
TIM, 16 Oct. 1937
COL, 31 Oct. 1937 (Photo).

1941 Mar. Vancouver
Sarah the Sea Hag stranded on Kitsilano Beach
W.A.Clemens and I.McTaggart-Cowan identified
it as a shark.
PROV, 5 Mar. 1941.

1947 Dec. Vernon Bay, Barkley Sound, Vancouver Is.
45-ft long, 145 vertebrae, 6" across
another shark
Seattle *Post Intelligencer*, 7 Dec. 1947
COL, 9 Dec. 1947.

1950 Delake, Oregon
four-ft across, four hairless tapering tails,
thick hair; no separate head.
expert says whale shark
TIM, 7 Mar. 1950.

1956 Dry Harbor, south of Yakutat, Alaska
100-ft long carcass, 15 ft wide
reddish-brown two-inch-long hair
syrupy blood, large teeth, crimson flesh rapidly decomposing.
Trevor Kincaid quoted: "description fits no known
creature"; W.A. Clemens says Baird's whale
Daily Empire, Juneau
Life Magazine, 8 Jun. 1956.
John Grissim, *National Fisherman*, Jun. 1991.

1962 Apr. Ucluelet
14-ft long, head like elephant
dragged ashore by Simon Peter
thought to be elephant seal
SUN, 14 Apr. 1962.

1963 Sep. Oak Harbor, Whidbey Is.,
20" skull "resembling a horse"
spine 6" in diameter; A.D.Welander, U of W Fisheries
thinks it's a basking shark
Whidbey News Times, 3 Oct. 1963 (Photos).

1968 Aug. De Courcy Is., W.Hagelund
Baby Caddy caught
W.Hagelund, 1987; *Whalers No More,* Harbour
Publishing, Madeira Park, B.C.

1991 Jul. Johns Is (San Juan Islands); Phyllis Harsh
small (< 2 ft) baby Caddy returned to water.
Interview by ELB, 26 Aug. 1993.

FOOTNOTES

INTRODUCTION
1. Heuvelmans, B., 1982.
2. Courtenay-Latimer, M., 1979, or Smith, J.L.B.,1956.
3. Taylor *et al.*, 1983.
4. Vu Van Dong *et al.*, 1993.
5. Ellis, R. 1994, pp. 113 ff.
6. Shackley, M.,1983, p.18.

CHAPTER I
1. LeBlond, P.H. and J. Sibert, 1973, p. 27.
2. Ellis, D.W. and L. Swan, 1981, p.98.
3. Reimer, W. 1993.
4. White, H., 1994.
5. Fladmark, K.R. *et al.*,1987.
6. Vancouver *Sun*, 19 Apr. 1952.
7. Vancouver *Province*, 24 Aug. 1940, p.5.
8. There are no villages by the name of Caedoo and three by the name of Kaidju (or Qai'dju) mentioned in Dalzell (1981). One of these is on the south side of Moore Channel which gives into Englefield Bay, on the west side of Moresby Is.; another is in the extreme southeast of Moresby Is., near Benjamin Pt., facing Hecate Strait; the third is on the ocean side of Kunghit Is., just north of Gilbert Bay. Of the three sites, the one most likely to experience calm seas and be a safe port of call for two men in a small boat is the second.

9. Mattison, D., 1964. Mattison's article is based on: Osmond Fergusson, "Abstract of daily notes taken during prospecting trip in the Queen Charlotte Islands, June 26th 1897." Newcombe Family Papers, BC Archives and Records Service, Add. Mss. 1077, v.20, file 2.
10. LeBlond, P.H. and J. Sibert, *ibid.*, p.9.
11. Heuvelmans, B., 1968, p. 445.
12. *Victoria Daily Times*, 19 Oct. 1933.
13. LeBlond, P.H. and J. Sibert, *ibid.*, p 10.
14. *Victoria Daily Times*, 17 Oct. 1933, p.1.
15. White, H., *ibid.*

CHAPTER II
1. *Victoria Daily Times*, 5 Oct. 1933, p.1.
2. *Victoria Daily Times*, 24 Oct. 1933, p.1.
3. *Victoria Daily Times*, 11 Oct. 1933, p.15.
4. The original letter is in Archie Wills' scrapbook of Caddy clippings.
5. *Victoria Daily Colonist*, 17 Oct.1933, p.1. Completely ignoring Cadborosaurus or Caddy, the *Colonist* suggested Amy as a friendlier name for the sea-monster than Seattle's proposal of "Old Hiaschuckaluck" (which we recognize as a variant of the Manhousat *hiyitl'iik*).
6. *Victoria Daily Times*, 23 Oct. 1933, p.1.
7. *Victoria Daily Times*, 21 Oct. 1933, p.1.
8. *Victoria Daily Times*, 7 Oct. 1933, p.2. The editorialist clearly uses the word mammal to denote any large animal, rather than in its more precise zoological meaning.
9. Vancouver *Sun*, 18 Oct. 1933, p.1.
10. A copy of G.P. Wilson's letter, undated, is included in Archie Wills' scrapbook.
11. *New York Herald Tribune*, 17 Oct. 1933, p.1.
12. *Victoria Daily Times*, 17 Oct. 1933, p.1.
13. *Victoria Daily Colonist*, 18 Oct .1933.
14. *Victoria Daily Times*, 10 Oct.1933, p.1.
15. *Victoria Daily Times*, 17 Oct. 1933, p.2.
16. *Victoria Daily Times*, 21 Oct. 1933.
17. *Victoria Daily Times*, *ibid.* A whole page of the Saturday edition was devoted to a discussion of what Caddy might be.
18. *Victoria Daily Times*, 10 Oct. 1933, p.2.

19. *Victoria Daily Times*, 11 Oct. 1933, p.4.
20. For example, he wrote an extensive description of the discovery and naming of Caddy in the *Illustrated London News*, 6 Jan. 1934.
21. Letter of Archie Wills to P.H. LeBlond, 13 May 1970.
22. Bousfield, E.L. and P.H. LeBlond, 1995.

CHAPTER III
1. Vancouver *Sun*, 6 Dec. 1933, p.20.
2. *Victoria Daily Times*, 23 Jan. 1934, p.1.
3. *Victoria Daily Times*, 9 Jan. 1934, p.1.
4. *Victoria Daily Times*, 21 Nov. 1950.
5. Vancouver *Province*, 29 Sep. 1947.
6. Vancouver *Province*, 19 Nov. 1940, p.23.
7. Letter to E.L. Bousfield, 24 Aug. 1993.
8. LeBlond, P.H. and J. Sibert, *ibid.*, p. 24.
9. LeBlond,P.H. and J. Sibert, *ibid.*, p. 12.
10. *Victoria Daily Times*, 14 Feb.1953, p.1.
11. Letter to P.H. LeBlond, 22 Jul. 1985.
12. Letter and telephone conversations with P.H. LeBlond , July 1971.
13. Vancouver *Sun*, 8 Jan. 1934, p.1.
14. Vancouver *Province*, 3 Jul. 1941, p.7.
15. Letter to P.H. LeBlond, 9 Mar. 1988.
16. *Victoria Daily Colonist*, 2 Dec. 1950.
17. *Victoria Daily Colonist*, 22 Jul. 1951.
18. Letter to P.H. LeBlond, 9 Nov. 1989.
19. LeBlond, P.H. and J. Sibert, *ibid.*, p. 25.
20. *Victoria Daily Times*, 30 Dec. 1962.
21. Vancouver *Province*, 17 Apr. 1936, p.1.
22. *Sidney Review*, 12 Sep. 1934.
23. *Sidney Review*, 29 Mar. 1961.
24. Vancouver *Province*, 14 Jan. 1943, p.1.
25. Victoria *Times-Colonist*, 28 Jul. 1993, p.1.
26. Vancouver *Province*, 8 Dec. 1938, p.1.
27. Vancouver *Province*, 31 Mar. 1939.
28. *Advance*, Langley, B.C., 22 Apr. 1960, p.1.
29. Victoria *Times-Colonist*, 31 Jul. 1993, p.1.
30. Letter to E.L. Bousfield, 20 Aug. 1992.
31. *Pacific Northwest*, Seattle, Apr. 1993, p. 30-34.

CHAPTER IV
1. *Daily Alaska Empire*, 28 Nov. 1930, p.1.
2. *Fairbanks Daily News Miner*, 28 Nov. 1930.
3. Vancouver *Province*, 22 Nov. 1934, p.1. A personal account of the discovery appeared under Dr. Carter's signature in the *Province* on Nov. 23.
4. *New York Herald Tribune*, 23 Nov. 1934, p.1.
5. Vancouver *Sun*, 23 Nov. 1934, p.9.
6. Vancouver *Sun*, 26 Nov. 1934, p.1.
7. *New York Times*, 26 Nov. 1934, p.17.
8. Corley-Smith,P., 1989, p.45.
9. Vancouver *Sun*, 26 Nov. 1934, p.1.
10. Heuvelmans, B. 1968, p.134.
11. Vancouver *Province*, 5 Mar. 1941, p 15.
12. *Ibid.*
13. Vancouver *Sun*, 8 Dec. 1947.
14. Heuvelmans, B., 1968, p. 475.
15. *Whidbey News Times*, 3 Oct. 1963, p.1.
16. *Victoria Daily Colonist* 8, Oct. 1936.
17. Letter to W.A. Clemens, Director, Institute of Oceanography, University of B.C., from G.C. Carl, Director, B.C. Provincial Museum. (dated 17 Dec.1956).
18. This photo (BC Provincial Archives catalogue number HP 52840; Negative No. H-4767) appeared in the *Victoria Daily Colonist* on 31 Oct. 1937 and in the Vancouver *Sun*, 5 May 1960.
19. Page 11 of what are probably the original photographer's notes penciled on a pad of 3" x 5.5" paper stapled to the inside back cover of an album entitled "Photos by Mr G.V. Boorman, First-aid Officer, The Consolidated Whaling Corp. Ltd., Rose Harbour, Queen Charlotte Islands." The photos of interest are No. 37 and 38, on page 7. Clippings from the Vancouver *Sun* and Vancouver *Province* (16 Oct. 1937) are glued to the back of the previous page. The album itself consists of seven 8.5" x 11" pages; hand-written inked explanations of the photos reproduce the penciled notes, except for small variants. An important variant is that the word Baleana has been inserted in parentheses after the word horse in "...a tail similar to that of a horse." It is likely that that word has been inserted following the quote about "the tail resembling a single blade of gill bone as found in whales' jaws" from the *Fisheries Bulletin* (#21, below).

20. Hagelund, W., 1987, p.177.
21. *Fisheries News Bulletin*, Vol VIII, No. 95, Dept. Fisheries, Ottawa, Sep 1937, p.2.
22. Vancouver *Province*, 23 Jul. 1937.
23. Bousfield, E.L. and P.H. LeBlond, 1995, *ibid.*
24. Hagelund, W. *ibid.*, p.178.
25. E.L. Bousfield interviewed Phyllis Harsh on Johns Island on 26 Sep. 1992, in the company of Craig Staude, of Friday Harbor Marine Laboratories.

CHAPTER V
1. *Victoria Daily Times*, 9 Oct. 1969, p. 21.
2. *Victoria Daily Times*, 75th Anniversary Supplement, 8 Jun. 1959, p.12.
3. *Victoria Daily Times*, 17 Oct. 1933, p. 2.
4. *Victoria Daily Times*, 15 Nov. 1933.
5. Victoria *Times-Colonist*, 29 Jun. 1981, p 11.
6. *Victoria Daily Times*, 16 Apr. 1951.
7. *Victoria Daily Times*, 21 Oct .1952.
8. *Ibid.*
9. *Victoria Daily Times*, 8 Dec. 1947.
10. *Victoria Daily Times*, 30 May 1963.
11. *Victoria Daily Times*, 28 Mar. 1952, p.1.
12. *Victoria Daily Times*, 1 Apr. 1952.
13. *Victoria Daily Times*, May 1963.

CHAPTER VI
1. Vancouver *Province*, 9 Mar. 1943, p.1.
2. Vancouver *Sun*, 25 Feb. 1954.
3. Heuvelmans,B., 1968, p.552.
4. Thomson, R.E. 1981, Chapters 10-14.
5. M.Johnson, call to E.L.Bousfield, Aug. 1993.
6. McGowan, 1994, Ch. 11, discusses propulsion mechanisms of marine animals.
7. Weddell seals and elephant seals can reach depths of over 1,000 metres and stay under for up to two hours, a period which exceeds by three or four times the time required to deplete all their oxygen supply. The conclusion is that their physiology adapts to a specially low oxygen consumption level during deep dives. (See LeBoeuf *et al.*, 1988).

Footnotes

8. For example, Heuvelmans, B. 1968, p. 553.
9. Dunson, W.A., 1975.
10. B.A.Block *et al.*, 1993.
11. Peter W. Hochachka, at the University of British Columbia, has studied physiological responses to low oxygen, cold conditions faced by deep-diving animals. For more information on this subject, see his paper in *Science*, 1986.
12. An application of the classification of organisms in terms of primitive versus advanced traits may be found in Jarrett and Bousfield, 1994.
13. Buffetaut, E.,1983.

CHAPTER VII
1. As quoted by Heuvelmans, B., 1968, p. 393; see also Garner, B.S., 1976, p.65.
2. The famous 1934 surgeon's photo of Nessie was recently claimed to be a hoax; some of the photos claiming to show Ogopogo are clearly pictures of intersecting wave groups.
3. A careful interpretation of the Latin version of St. Columba's life shows that the encounter with a large animal did NOT occur in Loch Ness, but at a crossing of the River Ness, and may not be related at all to the animal now known as Nessie. (Thomas, C., 1988). Comprehensive overviews of the Nessie phenomenon are found in Mackal, R., 1976, and Campbell, S., 1986. A succinct review of acoustic measurements and underwater photography in Loch Ness is also found in McGowan, C., 1976.
4. For information on Ogopogo, cf. Gaal, A., 1986.
5. The Storsjöodjuret (The Great Lake Monster) is described in a pamphlet written by Ulla Oscarsson, available from the Jömtland County Museum, Sweden. ISBN 91-85390-95-X.
6. Observations of Champ are summarized in Zarzynski, J., 1984.

BIBLIOGRAPHY

Block, B.A., J.R. Finnerty, A.F.R. Stewart, J. Kidd, 1963. "Evolution of endothermy in fish: mapping physiological traits on a molecular phylogeny." *Science*, 260, 210-213.

Bousfield, E.L. and P.H. LeBlond, 1995. "An account of *Cadborosaurus willsi*, new genus, new species, a large aquatic reptilian form from the Pacific Coast of North America." *Amphipacifica*, 1, Supplement 1.

Buffetaut, E.,1983. "Vertical flexure in Jurassic and Cretaceous marine crocodilians and its relevance to modern 'sea serpent' reports." *Cryptozoology*, 2, 85-89.

Campbell, S., 1986. *The Loch Ness Monster: The Evidence*. Aquarian Press, Wellingborough, Northamptonshire.

Corley-Smith, P., 1989. *White Bears and Other Curiosities: The First Hundred Years of the Royal British Columbia Museum*. Royal B.C. Museum, Victoria.

Courtenay-Latimer, M., 1979. "My story of the first coelacanth." In: J.E. McCosher and M.D. Lagos, Eds. *The Biology and Physiology of the Living Coelacanth*. California Academy of Science Occasional Paper No. 134: 6-10.

Dalzell, K.E., 1981. *The Queen Charlotte Islands, Vol.2, Places and Names*. Bill Ellis Publisher, Queen Charlotte City.

Dunson, W.A., 1975. Editor. *The Biology of Sea Snakes.* University Park Press, Baltimore.

Ellis, D.W. and L. Swan, 1981. *Teachings of the Tides.* Theytus Books Ltd. Nanaimo, B.C.

Ellis, R., 1994. *Monsters of the Sea.* A.Knopf, New York.

Fladmark, K.R., D.E. Nelson,T.A. Brown, J.S. Vogel and J.R. Southon, 1987. "AMS dating of two wooden artifacts from the northwest coast." *Canadian Journal of Archaeology*, 11, 1-12.

Gaal, A., 1986. *Ogopogo.* Hancock House, Surrey, B.C.

Garner, B.S., 1976. *Canada's Monsters.* Potlatch Publ. Hamilton, Ont.

Hagelund, W., 1987. *Whalers No More.* Harbour Publishing, Madeira Park, B.C.

Heuvelmans, B., 1968. *In the Wake of the Sea-Serpents.* Hill & Wang, New York.

Heuvelmans, B., 1982. "What is cryptozoology." *Cryptozoology*, 1: pp. 1-12.

Hochachka, P.W., 1986. "Defense Strategies Against Hypoxia and Hypothermia", *Science*, 17 Jan. 1986, 231, pp. 234-241.

Jarrett, N.E., and E.L. Bousfield, 1994. "The amphipod superfamily Phoxocephaloidea on the Pacific coast of North America. Part 1. Metharpiniinae, new subfamily." *Amphipacifica*, 1, No.1, pp. 58-140.

LeBlond, P.H. and J. Sibert, 1973. "Observations of large unidentified marine animals in British Columbia and adjacent waters." Manuscript Report 28, Institute of Oceanography, University of British Columbia.

Le Boeuf, B.J., D.P. Costa, A.C. Huntley and S.D. Feldkamp, 1988. *Canadian Journal of Zoology*, 66, 446-458.

Mackal, R.,1976. *The Monsters of Loch Ness*. Swallow Press, Chicago.

Mattison, D., 1964. "An 1897 Sea Serpent Sighting in the Queen Charlotte Islands." *B.C.Historical News*, Vol 17, No. 2, p. 15.

McGowan, C., 1976. "The search for the Loch Ness phenomena." *Rotunda*, 9, No. 2, 19-25.

McGowan, C., 1994. *Diatoms to Dinosaurs*. Island Press/Shearwater Books, Washington, D.C.

Nash, O., 1959. *Verses from 1929 On*. Little, Brown. Boston.

Norman, D., 1985. *The Illustrated Encyclopaedia of Dinosaurs*. Crescent Books, New York.

Reimer, W., 1993. "Mary Clifton, Comox Elder." pp. 10-12 in *Gulf Islands Guardian*, Vol 2, No 4. Spring 1993.

Shackley, M., 1983. *Wildmen*. Thames & Hudson, London.

Smith, J.L.B.,1956. *Old Fourlegs: The Story of the Coelacanth*. Longmans, Green, London.

Taylor, L.R., L.J.V. Campagno and P.J. Struhsaker, 1983. "Megamouth - a new species, genus, and a new family of lamnoid sharks (*Megachasmia pelagios*, Family Megachasmidae) from the Hawaiian Islands." Proc. Calif. Acad. Sci., 43: 87-110.

Thomas, C., 1988. "The 'monster' episode in Adomnan's life of St. Columba." *Cryptozoology*, 7, 38-45.

Thomson, R.E. 1981. *Oceanography of the British Columbia Coast, Canada*. Fisheries and Aquatic Sciences Special Publication No.56, 291 pp. Queen's Printer, Ottawa.

Vu Van Dong, Pham Mong Giao, Nguyen Ngoc Chinh, Do Tuoc, Peter Arctander and John Mackinnon, 1993. "A new species of living bovid from Vietnam." *Nature*, 363: 443-445.

White, H., 1994. "The Cadborosaurus meets Hubert Evans.", *Raincoast Chronicles Six/Ten*, Collector's Edition II. pp. 276-278, Harbour Publishing, Madeira Park, BC.

Wyss, A.R., 1989. "Flippers and pinniped phylogeny: has the problem of convergence been overrated?" *Marine Mammal Science*, Vol 5, No 4, 343-360.

Zarzynski, J., 1984. *Champ - Beyond the Legend*. Bannister Publ.

INDEX

Ackman, Capt. T., 118
Alexander, W., 99
Altman, C., 37, 106
ambergris, 50
Anderson, C., 101
Anderson, E., 116
Anderson, P., 13, 96
Andrews, C., 27-32, 83, 98, 99
Andrews, D., and C., 109
Architeuthis (see kraken)
Aun, H., 118
Avery, R.E. Jr., 114
Bain, Capt. G.S., 116
Ball, C., 70
Barker, J.M., 94
basking shark, 47, 50
Batchelor, G., 84
Beattie, W.J., 105
Behaviour of
Cadborosaurus
chasing birds, 29, 31, 40
diving, 2, 10, 38, 40
feeding, 30, 40, 78
on land, 42
reproduction, 80
respiration, 78
swimming, 35, 40, 76
voice/blow, 40
Belcher, Mrs. C., 101
Bellamy, D., 98
Berends, D., 40, 118

Biscoe, Mrs. F., 100
Biscaro, C.O., 103
Bjork, S., 115
Body features of
Cadborosaurus
colour, 71
distinguishing features, 71
eyes, 12, 32, 33, 39, 57
ears/horns, 10, 34, 35, 36, 37, 39
flippers, 32, 43
hair, 38, 39
head- snake-like, 8, 31, 38
giraffe-like, 10, 11, 37
horse-like, 13, 32, 34, 37,42
cow-like, 38
hot or cold blooded? 79
humps or coils, 2, 11, 29, 34, 37, 42
long neck, 2, 10, 11, 35, 38, 43
mane, 2,35, 38
mouth, 29, 32, 37, 39
smell, 43
tail, 32, 43
Boorman, G.V., 48, 52, 55
Bradley, Mrs. H., 108

Bromley, S., 117
Brown, B., 46
Brown, J.T., and family, 108
Bryden, R.H., 20, 98
Burgess, C., 103
Burniston, D., 101
Burt-Martin, Mrs., 104
Butler, Mrs. D.,108
Cadborosaurus
Amy, 20, 63
as sea-lion family, 65, 70
baby specimen, 57, 59, 80
captured, 64, 66
early synthesis, 24
modern diagnostic, 81
family, 42
frequency of sightings, 27
habitat, 72
hypotheses for discovery, 90
naming, 18, 60
as familiar marine animals, 70
Penda, 30, 70
Cadger, E., 100
Cameron family, 112
Carcasses
Gambier Island, 50
Henry Island, 46, 120

Index

Naden Harbour, 50, 76, 82, 120
  photos, 52, 53
  compared to other animals, 54
  others, 121
Valdez, Alaska, 45, 120
Vernon Bay, 49, 121
Vancouver, 48, 121
Whidbey Island, 49, 121
Carl, C., 49, 64, 70
Carter, N., 46, 119
Celona, J. and M., 43, 117
Champ, 2, 85, 87
Chilton, J.W., 31, 99
Christensen, H., 103
Clark, Mrs. E.M., 97
Clarke, Mr. and Mrs. W.G., 113
Clemens, W.A., 47, 48, 120
Cobert, Mrs. R., 49
Cockburn,R.D., 35, 110
coelacanth, ix, 2
Cole, Mrs. C.K., 100
Cole, C.Q., 116
Coleman, G., 108
Collins, Mrs. A.W., 104
Conrod, Mrs. T., 113
Cook, C.G. 11, 95
Cooney, Mrs. P., 118
Corbet, F., 116
Corner, J., 107
Crawford, C.P., 35, 110
Cryptozoology, ix
Dailey, J., 110
Dalton, Mr. and Mrs. C.F., 111
Dawe, A.P., and Mrs. 40, 100
Devlin, W., 102
De Witz-Krebs, S. von, 111
Didsbury, Mr. and Mrs., 38, 109
Duesenbury, R., 32, 103
Dumaresq, S., 99

Eagles, C.F., 20, 98
Easson, J.S., 104
Elliott, R.M., 11, 95
Ellisas, F., 96
Erickson, N., 34, 111
Evans, H., 13, 97
Ewert, R. and W., 115
Fannin, J., 47
Fergusson, O., 8, 9, 94
Finn John, 55
Fisher, Mrs., 104
Forbes, Mrs. H., 11, 95
Foster, Mrs. W.S., 114
Fraser, E., 97
Fraser, C. McLean, 23
Gaetz, R., 42, 102
Gannonx, J., 102
Garcin, A.D., 51
Garner, O.J. and R., 116
Garvie, W.L., 105
Georgeson, N., 27-29, 98
Georgeson, K., 30, 31, 98
Gibson, W. and Mrs., 40, 104
Gibson, C., 45
Gilstein, Mrs. A., 113
Goff, G., 115
Grant, S., 115
Grant, D., 118
Grant, W.B., 95
Green, R., 118
Green, E., 102
Grist, Mrs. S.H., 105
Guy, Mrs. R., 39, 113
Hagelund, W., 50, 57, 80, 89, 121
Harsh, Mrs. P., 59, 80, 117, 121
Hayes, H.A. Jr., 105
Hegelson, R.R., 107
Henderson, S., 112
Heppell, E., 108
Hergt, C., 114
Heuvelmans, B., ix, 48, 49, 74, 83
Hewett, G., 116
Higgs, W.Y., 42, 101
Hinde, W.F., 103

Hiyitl'iik/ Hiaschuckaluck, 4, 23, 47
Hobbs, Mr. and Mrs. S.M., 110
Hodgson, T., 102
Holland, Mrs., K.B., 39, 113
Homewood, R.E. and Mrs., 105
Hooper, Mrs. D., 18, 97
House, Capt., 106
Huband, F.S., 51, 55
Hunt, W. and I., 35, 100
Ingram, N., 103
Jackson, M., 99, 106
Jamieson, Mr., 102
Johnson, A.E., 96
Johnson, M., 111
Johnston, H.R. 107
Kavande, O., 100
Kemp, F.W., 15, 23, 64, 97
Kemperlink, G., 111
Kennedy, W., 38, 112
Kermode, F., 23, 47, 49, 56-57
Kilner, K., 116
Kincaid, T., 23, 47, 120
Kinloch, R., 106
kraken, x
Kutz, R.E. and family, 114
Landstrom, Capt., 99
Langley, W.H., 15, 64, 97
Langton, B., 117
Lawton, F.E., 104
Layfield, J., 103
Lebel, Mrs. M., 95
Leighton, Mrs. R.H., 107
Lind, J., 101
Liston,T., 38, 103
Loach, R., 35, 110
Loch Ness, 14, 63, 85
Lovvold, E., 103
Lynch, T. and E., 99
Macfarlane, G.R., 42, 101
Mackal, R., 85
Marsh, C., and E., 31, 99
Marshall, F., 42, 102

Martin, M., 115
Mason, J., 108
Maycock, F., 108
McAllister, 97
McAndrew, Mrs., 105
McCord, M., 111
McCurdy, W.R., 114
Macdonald, P., 114
McDonald, W.J., 45
McGavin, I., 99
McIntyre, J., 38, 109
McKay, E., 99
McKay, G.O., 106
McPhelan, F., 106
McTaggart-Cowan, I., 48, 57, 120
megamouth shark, x
Menzies, R., 103
merhorse, 72, 73, 83
Meynell, family, 101
Miller, D., 38, 112
Minchin, R. and wife, 118
Mitchell, B., 109
Molberg, A., 116
Monrufet, J., 112
Morgan, D., 105
Morley, B., 109
Morton, R., 102
Murray, J.F., 96
Navy officer, 31, 108
Neil, G., 98
Nilsen, Mrs. D., 106
Nord, J., 13, 96
Numkse lee Kwala, 5
Oban, B., 96
Obman, Capt., 96
Ogopogo, 2, 61, 64, 85, 87
O'Leary, J., 45
Olson, H., 98
Oosterhoof, J., 111
Osland, T., 42, 117
Owens, R., 70
Painton, Mrs. D.W., 109
Palmer, R., 109
Pantages, P. and H., 37, 106
Parkyn, G.F., 29, 30
Parris, R., 102

Parson, Mrs. F., 2
Pattullo, T.D., 63
Pearson, F., 114
Pender, A., 30, 31, 98, 99
Peter, Simon, 120
petroglyph 5, 6
Philips, J. 11
plesiosaur, 22, 48, 82, 107
Plimley, T. and wife, 105
Pratley, W., 103
Prengel, Capt. W., 21, 98
Probert, R.E., 114
Read, W.F., 104
Reeve, H. 13, 97
Rendall, B., 96
Rhodo, E. and husband, 104
Richardson, J., 21
Roberts, M., 66
Rodgers, Ruth and husband, 118
Ross, Miss Nettie, 66
Russell, J., 70
Sagar, H., 99
Saggers, G.W., 107
Salsbury, J., 110
Sanders, L., 115
Sandstrom, H., 46
Sarah the Sea Hag, 48, 120
Schaff, K. and husband, 115
Schwarz, H., 49
Scott, J., 113
sea-giraffe, 84, 86
Shaw, J., 42, 101
Sherwin, I., 33, 110
Shillito, W., 102
Sinclair, D., 43, 117
Skagit river atlatl, 6, 7
Smith, J., 100
Smith, J. and C., 111
Smith, R., 116
Smith, T. and M., 110
Smith, W., 42, 102
Sommerville, A., 105
Sowerby, P., 103
Spence, E.F., 110

Spencer, S. and Mrs., 104
Sprague, A.J., 96
Stacey, Mrs. A.R., 40, 112
Stanford, F., 110
Stannard, F., 8
Stephenson, E.J., 42, 100
Stephens, R., 13, 97
Stewart, A., 70
Stewart, Mr. and Mrs. R.A., 113
Storsjöodjuret, 85, 87
Stout, Mrs., M., 1, 112
Taylor, W.W., 100
T'chain-ko, 5
Thompson, G. and wife, 115
Thompson, J.N., 36, 115
Tickle, B., 108
Tildesley, Mrs. C.E., 102
Tillapaugh, L., 107
Timney, M., 117
Titus, L.H., 94
Tupper, M., 107
Vu Quang Ox, x
Wakefield, Mr. and Mrs. K., 108
Wakeford, J.W., 105
Wakelen, J., 51, 55, 56
Walker, J., 112
Warren, G.I., 65
Webb, A., 38, 112
Welander, A.D., 49, 121
Welch, P., 10, 95
Welham, Mr. and Mrs. D., 113
Wells, J., 40, 118
Whelan, H., 6
White, E., 98
Williams, M., 99
Wills, A., 17, 21, 25, 60, 91
Wilson, E., 112
Winkelman, R., 38, 106
Winship, H., 33, 110
Wragg, G., 101
Wyper, J.M., 110
Young, W., 106